The Competition Within

How Members Will Reinvent Associations

REBECCA ROLFES

iUniverse, Inc.
New York   Bloomington

The Competition Within

How Members Will Reinvent Associations

iUniverse books may be ordered through booksellers or by contacting:

iUniverse
1663 Liberty Drive
Bloomington, IN 47403
www.iuniverse.com
1-800-Authors (1-800-288-4677)

ISBN: 978-0-595-52695-6 (pbk)
ISBN: 978-0-595-51477-9 (cloth)
ISBN: 978-0-595-62749-3 (ebk)

Printed in the United States of America
iUniverse rev. date 2/18/09

TO IMAGINATION

in all senses of the word

The social state is at once so natural, so necessary, and so habitual to man that he never conceives himself otherwise than as a member of a body.

—John Stuart Mill

Contents

Why do people join associations? Is membership becoming irrelevant?

For most associations, core competencies still include research, meetings, advocacy, publishing, standards, and certification. Nothing has changed, but everything is new.

Can an association use the power of online community to create value? Will online communities replace associations?

It's time to rethink your value proposition. You can calculate customer lifetime value and the cost-benefit of membership.

Preface

My first experience working for an association was in Brussels as director of communications for The Conference Board Europe in the late 1980s and early 1990s. The job was to oversee public relations, the annual report, one newsletter, and some speech writing. The staff was tiny, and I got to do pretty much anything that needed doing. In those four years, I launched other newsletters and tried, as much as the limitations of print permitted, to segment the messages—to make them relevant to the readers. It wasn't a strategy so much as something that just seemed to make sense.

Fast forward to the mid 1990s: I was a founder of Imagination Publishing in the United States, and the company had just landed its first association client, the Illinois Bankers Association. Imagination was a start-up company, and it would produce anything for the IBA—publications, conference materials, print collateral. The IBA was small, but so were we, and we both learned a lot—they about the virtues and the challenges of outsourcing, we about working for a membership organization and how that differed from working for a for-profit.

It is now fifteen years later, and Imagination is now the parent company of Association Growth Partners. I've worked with fourteen associations, most of them business-to-business (B2Bs). I've made every one of those new business presentations and figured out what those associations needed—not just what they asked for, but what they actually needed. And this is what I now know: *associations now face competition, many of them for the first time, and they are not prepared for it.* Association leaders have worried for years about competition from for-profits—conference organizers, for instance. But now competitive pressure is so intense that a siege mentality pervades many associations.

The most recent and most important competitive force is the association members themselves. Online communities provide a new, instantaneous way to associate with like-minded people. They operate around the clock and with no fees attached.

People outside an association's home country who don't know or care about the carefully constructed brand. Young potential members who do most of their living, working, and communicating online. Tech-savvy entrepreneurs who see a market and know how to exploit it with new media and delivery systems. All of these groups are going after associations' bread and butter. The competition is not globalization, demographics, or technology. The competition is coming from within.

Rebecca Rolfes
Chicago, Illinois
November, 2008

Methodology

This book examines the competitive forces impacting business-to-business associations. There may be lessons here for consumer, cause-related, artistic, and philanthropic nonprofits as well, but the research for this book focused on B2B associations, both individual-member and trade organizations.

The research was conducted by the author and by Ali Rizvi, the research editor. Rizvi audited seventy-five B2B associations in the United States, Europe, and Asia, examining member benefits, core competencies, value propositions, and strategic initiatives. He also audited several associations of associations to expand the total number of entities examined to more than one hundred. Research reports and books were read, twenty interviews with association executives were conducted, and thirty-five associations were included based on speeches, white papers, or other published material. These research findings represent a snapshot in time and are not meant to be statistically significant.

Introduction

I've never been much of a joiner. Having one thing in common with a group of people and wanting to spend a lot of time together based on that single shared interest or life condition has always seemed very narrow to me. And once you've been president of the Newcomers' League of Indianapolis, Indiana, what more is there, anyway?

However, now that I have worked with many associations—mostly business-to-business trade and professional associations—I find that they are anything but narrow. The people who join are passionate about something—their jobs, their industry, their colleagues, or the ever-changing landscape of what they do. The commonalities are myriad; the range is enormous.

And yet, in many instances, these associations are under siege. Globalization and its attendant consolidation are cutting into trade association membership—fewer companies, fewer members. Globalization disperses professions; no single country has a monopoly on expertise. Careers are portable, and companies and individuals alike want services regardless of where they are. Potential members far from an association's headquarters want the same thing that those close to home want, and local, for-profit companies are ready to provide it. Additionally (and the reason for this book's title), individuals are starting their own "associations" online. These organizations often have no dues, no barriers to entry, and lots of opportunities to participate. Further, in many ways they are more relevant to individual members because the individuals are the ones creating the experience.

In 2005, the U.S. Chamber of Commerce released a study called *The Future of the Competitive Association*. The study set out to discover why associations grow and what separates fast-growing associations from slow-growing ones. At the end of that study, the author posed several questions that needed further study. One was, "Will globalization continue to add operational and competitive threats to associations as well as opportunities for those positioned for growth?"

Of course, the answer is yes. But globalization also adds complexity and richness to the already complex world of B2B associations. It is not something from which to run, but something to embrace. Mark Langley, a CPA and both executive vice president and chief operating officer of the Project Management Institute, says that globalization is irreversible. It is now a fact of many association's lives, at a minimum because it is part of their members' lives.

To their credit, many associations see globalization as an opportunity, not a threat. They do not minimize the challenges but refuse to operate as if under siege. Others want to pull up the drawbridge in the same way that protectionist legislation tries to stave off the inevitability of foreign competition.

As I wrote this book, I found that the siege mentality among associations comes not from globalization alone or from the threat of self-organized online community, but from an almost complete unfamiliarity with competition. An executive who was considering outsourcing her association's publication to my company said, "They have to advertise with us; we're the association."

"They," of course, don't have to do any such thing. The safe purview of being a household name in a given field is long gone. "They" can do whatever they want, go wherever they want, and take their advertising budget, membership dues, training needs, and conference registration with them. When they go, the most important thing they'll take will be their passion. Without the sustained, often intense commitment of its members, an association is nothing. The same altruistic energy that motivates people to edit Wikipedia entries fires associations, and in this Wiki-rich era, people don't have to pay dues to find a home for their passion.

Another association executive—more than one, in fact—told me, "My members don't go online." The usual rationale for this amazing assumption is that their members are old(er), and therefore uncomfortable with technology. In fact, most professionals are online every day, along with many millions of people who stay at home. They are all over the place on the Internet; they're just not on your association's site.

From a largely protected world where the only competition came from other nonprofits, associations have been catapulted into an intensely competitive environment. The world went global and high-tech in the blink of an eye, and many associations are still gasping for air in the backwash.

P.J. O'Rourke famously said that the Berlin Wall fell because no one wanted to wear ugly Bulgarian shoes. Technology let East Berliners see what the rest of the world had; it made the wall irrelevant. That's what globalization and technology are doing to associations. In a borderless world, smart people who are worth knowing live everywhere.

Without walls or borders, a siege mentality does no good. Millions of highly committed people support associations. Millions more find what they need in communities on Facebook or LinkedIn populated by people they've never met. Professionals on the other side of the world clamor for knowledge transfer that will build their economies, and plenty of for-profit education providers are ready to supply it. Those with knowledge to impart search for a platform, and social media provides the stage. No borders, no walls, and the seeds of change are as much within the membership as outside it. What's an association to do?

In the course of researching for this book, I also discovered why I don't join. After reading book after book on the subject and sitting in room after room filled with people whose sole job is to talk people into joining—people who spend their days figuring out what some demographic wants and will pay for—I finally saw that I never wanted a one-size-fits-all experience. It wasn't that I hated decoupage lessons in the Girl Scouts or had nothing much in common with my fellow Indianapolis newcomers. It wasn't that the experience was too narrow, but that it was too broad.

Call me picky or a slower study than I like to think, but the current world, the one without borders or walls, is made for people like me. I can get exactly, and I mean *exactly*, what I want—not what you have to sell. I can sit here or in Timbuktu, never interact with anyone, and have all my needs met—lonely and kind of sad, but possible. I want a membership made for me alone. The beautiful truth is that I *can* have that without being lonely or sad, and I *can* have it in Timbuktu.

Associations must figure out what I want and provide it to me however, wherever, and whenever I want it. In a borderless world powered by technology, that is not only possible, but easy. The competition has figured that out. Have you?

Chapter 1

Why Join?

Birds of a feather will gather together.

—**Robert Burton**

As taxis pull into Ushuaia, Argentina, a giant round sign greets visitors arriving from the airport. The sign welcomes them to the town at the bottom of the world in Tierra del Fuego, state of Patagonia, on behalf of Rotary International.

Along the two-lane blacktop near Patagonia, Arizona, United States, a section of scrub-lined highway has been adopted by the Patagonia-Sonoita Rotary Club.

Neither of these local chapters of the 1.2 million-member international association cares that the organization itself is headquartered in Evanston, Illinois, just north of Chicago and, in every sense, a world away. Rotary members are not joining an association in Illinois. They are joining entirely local groups of small business owners who get together for coffee, networking, and community service. They may or may not do anything concrete to help Rotary meet its major humanitarian goal of eradicating polio. But they know that, for small business owners anywhere, doing good things for the community and being personally acquainted with community leaders is good for business. Rotary helps them do that. In towns the size of Patagonia, Arizona (population eight hundred), it also becomes a pillar of the members' social lives.

As is often the case, an individual's motivation for joining may not be part of the association's core mission. Rotary's motto is, "Service Above Self," and its main objective is, "service—in the community, in the workplace, and throughout the world," according to their Web site.

We'd like to think that people join associations because of their mission, their higher purpose. Whether it is service to mankind or raising the bar for a given profession, support for an association's mission is what supposedly galvanizes membership. This is certainly true of philanthropic associations, but for B2B associations, the cost-benefit is a bit more mercenary.

People join an association because of a compelling value proposition. The payoff, personally or professionally, has to be there. What am I going to get if I join? In today's intensely competitive environment, the traditional association value proposition looks a lot less compelling.

When technology offers what author Clay Shirky calls "the power of organizing without organizations," why pay dues? When global markets are interested in one specific part of an association's offering and are totally unfamiliar with volunteering, how can associations afford to operate as they always have? When a younger generation changes the workplace by blending their private lives with their professional lives and managing them both from any device with a wireless connection, why join an association with rigid ideas about boundaries? The Internet is a vast place full of data. Surely the answer to whatever you seek can be found unprotected by a firewall. And as the clamor for open access mounts, the firewalls themselves may come down. What will associations have to offer then?

When social networks remove the overhead of running an organization (and thus the fees), when information floats freely, when like-minded individuals in any specific—sometimes *extremely* specific—area are only a click away, when people in a chat room do not care what time it is where you are, why tie yourself to an association where one size (or maybe a few) has to fit many?

The answer is almost identical from one association to the next: access to data; conferences, meetings, and educational offerings; the opportunity to join local chapters or special interest groups; advocacy in some form; and, in the case of B2B associations, standards and accreditation. These things, or some combination thereof, make up the association value proposition, the reason to join, vertical group by vertical group.

There also is a factor of "reverse polarity," according to *The Decision to Join*, a 2007 report from the American Society of Association Executives

(ASAE). "Individuals receive value, and for no additional cost their decision generates value for those who share a common bond." In order to understand associations and why individuals decide to join or not—or to join but not renew—the study points out the balancing act that is central to the value equation: "What's in it for me and for us?" It turns out that the benefits to the common good (of the profession, the field, the industry, mankind) only slightly outweigh the value of personal benefits. "The unity of personal benefits and benefits to the field are the Yin and the Yang of association management," says the study. "They are the complementary opposites on a spectrum of value."

If associations are to survive, they must figure out how to ensure that "us" remains more important than "me." Networking on LinkedIn is about finding a job, filling a position, or uncovering new business opportunities. And LinkedIn's new "Groups" application is tailor-made for like-minded people who want to associate and share knowledge. An online community of project managers on Facebook, formed outside the confines of the Project Management Institute (PMI), has much the same common-good motivation that draws people to the mother ship.

There has to be more to an association than the same-old, same-old if associations are to compete in this environment. Joining an association, buying into its slow, consensus-building pace, is being replaced by the ability to fulfill needs quickly. People are accustomed to having what they want soon after they realize they want it.

Long-range commitment is built on short-term satisfaction consistently delivered. An association's purview as the honest broker or the independent third party certainly has value, but the market will not wait for it on that account. "They don't care that we're an association," says Mahala Renkey, publisher of *PM Network* at PMI. "We have to move more quickly."

For PMI, the value proposition is, "Making project management indispensable to business results." Translation: "Joining this association will make you indispensable. It will sell your worth within your organization and it will link what you do to the organization's bottom line. Therefore, project management will become how your company does what it does." PMI's value proposition sells the association to the intended member, the project manager, but it also sells "up" within the organization, appealing to decision makers focused on the bottom line.

The Institute of Food Technologists (IFT) changed its mission in 2008 to "Sharing sound science to ensure there is safe and abundant food for everyone." That meant developing a value proposition for global participation. The crucial change was "everyone," not simply people in the United States.

The opportunity became much bigger, but so did the number of potential competitors.

Fulfilling a value proposition no longer necessarily starts with membership. Associations now reap less than 40 percent of their revenues from dues. As that percentage declined over the last fifty years (precipitously over the last ten), associations went on the hunt for non-dues revenue. That focused largely on trying to sell members other things—books, education, standards, etc. The value proposition was still built on membership with a greater emphasis on cross-selling.

That tactic has gone as far as it can go. There is a limit to the number of standards and certifications that can be developed without cheapening the process. There also is a limit to how many related things the same group of people will buy. But further, the realities of globalization and technology mean that associations now are trying to sell things in the absence of membership. They no longer are able to simply cross-sell but must go into individual product sales. Rather than relying on dues to form a financial base, they lead with programs and services of interest to new markets. This enables buyers to short-circuit the slowness of associations. They can buy what they want and leave.

Half of the certified Project Management Professionals (PMPs) in the world are no longer members of PMI. They "bought" the certification by joining. Mark Langley, executive vice president and chief operating officer of PMI, says, "We will never go away from the membership model. It's almost a core principle with us." Despite this, in the future, associations will have to decide whether membership is necessary in every transaction.

"What I think will happen is that membership will go by the wayside and we'll go to an affiliation model," says Peter J. O'Neil, certified association executive (CAE) and assistant executive director of the American Industrial Hygiene Association. "They won't join. They'll affiliate. They'll attend a program."

Revenues from individual product sales are smaller, of course, but so is the risk, and the potential exists to court members when the time is right. Such unbundling puts associations firmly in step with author Chris Anderson's famous "long tail," selling more and more of less and less. Groups break into chunks, a process that is universally painful for organizations that have always been about unity.

Many associations correctly divine their members' latent needs to create products and services and thus provide value well outside the traditional bounds of membership. The *Future of the Competitive Association* study from the U.S. Chamber of Commerce focuses on opportunities within the association's "ecosystem" but outside of its existing membership.

For example, the American Heart Association provides downloadable heart-healthy shopping lists for easy use at the grocery store. The core membership (physicians) benefits because the shopping lists function as patient education, reduce the number of calls to the office and, as patients eat better, reduce the number of office visits. Also, the U.S. Chamber of Commerce launched a magazine for tort lawyers when it realized that the high cost of tort was a major cost of doing business for its members. Neither of these examples sends direct dollars to the bottom line, but both tighten the tie of members to organizations that are responsive and proactive.

Such divination increasingly will depend on field research, something associations have never done. Given that the members *are* the association, the organization has always felt that responsiveness was automatic. That no longer is the case. The world is more complex, the problems professionals face are more complicated, and choices are too numerous to mention. Figuring out the solution depends on correctly identifying the problem. By doing field research and by riding along with members—and perhaps more important, nonmembers—on the job, associations can begin to get to the real issues and create much more compelling value propositions and much more immediate stand-alone products and services than they currently offer.

JOINING THE FLOCK

One of sociology's ongoing quests is to discover whether taste determines personal connections or vice versa. Do we join the flock because we look like some of the birds or do we come to look like them once we join?

This dynamic can be seen at any association gathering. Go to a meeting of the Metals Service Center Institute and you will be in a room full of affluent, middle-aged white males from North America. There are a few women and a few members of various ethnic groups, but diversity is a struggle for this almost one-hundred-year-old, resolutely North American association in a mature industry. Go to a conference of the National Association of Corporate Directors and you'll find women and men in almost equal numbers, all conservatively dressed and most with degrees in law or economics.

Membership in any group is self-selecting. But what happens when an association goes global, for instance? Will the largely middle-aged membership of one nationality be replicated by an equally middle-aged group somewhere else? Will the membership still be mostly male or mostly middle managers or mostly from companies with less than $100 million in sales?

Jon Kleinberg, a computer science professor at Cornell University, investigated three things in his 2006 paper, "Group Formation in Large Social Networks: Membership, Growth and Evolution."

1. What influences someone to join a community?
2. What makes a community grow?
3. How do communities that overlap change over time?

The findings show that individuals join and a community grows based on the underlying network structure. "The tendency of an individual to join a community is influenced not just by the number of friends he or she has within the community, but also crucially by how those friends are connected to one another," Kleinberg writes. It is very much the fulfillment of the Arab proverb, "the friend of my friend is my friend."

The American Society for Quality (ASQ) followed its large corporate members overseas for obvious reasons. In 1997, its board began to pressure the sixty-one-year-old association. "[The board] said, 'My organization and my suppliers are all over the world and I want you to serve them the same way you serve me,'" says Paul Borawski, executive director and chief strategy officer. But the reason ASQ's globalization efforts have succeeded was the underlying network structure.

As a company expands to new markets, its employees constitute the "underlying network structure" of Kleinberg's research. Because they know each other and know people who know each other, they are more likely to join. They are also more likely to look alike and think alike. Being hired by IBM, for instance, demands certain skill sets and experience but also certain personality traits and cultural preferences. IBM employs the largest number of PMI members. As a result, wherever IBM goes, so goes PMI.

For smart associations looking to remain competitive, this means talking up within organizations. The value proposition cannot stop at the individual member's door. Associations must be more hooked in to where companies are going and therefore to the underlying network of the potential members they house. They also must expand their definition of "cultural relevance" beyond translation. The obvious as well as the latent needs of a new global market offer plentiful opportunities for associations who know how to capitalize on them.

In his paper, Kleinberg asks whether changes in membership precede or follow changes in interest. Do members from other countries ask to join an association first, or are the existing members interested in nondomestic issues and that drives the desire for international members? The data is less clear on this but suggests that trust trumps information as a motivation for new members. As membership changes to include people outside the headquarters country, those people have their own networks of trusted contacts that might also join. IFT's reputation for sound food science (and hence, food safety) drew the Chinese Institute of Food Science and Technology to ask the

American IFT to host symposiums in China. Information was important, but trust was the deciding factor.

A company in The Netherlands does business with a company in Brazil. People get to know each other, trust each other, and want to form mutually beneficial networking arrangements. A trade association is a convenient place to do that—the place where the supply meets the demand face-to-face. And once the association has a foothold in Brazil, the contacts of those new members bring in other members. Since the information needs of those members are being met simultaneously, it is difficult to separate the group's two motivations—trust and information.

Trust also makes associations fertile ground for online communities. The self-selected group of members and the related group of interested nonmembers would rather belong to an organization they can trust. Enabling those communities is another huge opportunity for associations willing to relinquish the illusion of control and embrace the possibilities.

HAPPIER AND MORE SUCCESSFUL

"Social capital" is the sociological term for advantage. People who do better are better connected; they have social capital. Pierre Bourdieu, an author of the concept, writes, "Social capital is the sum of the resources, actual or virtual, that accrue to an individual or group by virtue of possessing a durable network of more or less institutionalized relationships or mutual acquaintance and recognition."

Information flows more freely and more quickly within a network of acquaintances, and that yields advantage. Members of the network are more likely to trust each other. Productivity is higher given the tighter and more frequent communication that takes place almost behind closed doors.

"Associations are where the winners meet." That amazing statement comes from a study by The William E. Smith Institute for Association Research (*Where the Winners Meet*, 2008). People who belong to an association are better off, happier, and more successful than those who don't. Joining an association does not, of course, guarantee a happy, prosperous life—if only it were that easy. Rather, the reverse is true. People join associations because they are happy and successful. Associations offer a place for them to identify themselves, form mutually beneficial relationships with their peers, and access information. By offering those opportunities, associations gain high-value members. And following Kleinberg's findings, high-value members attract other members.

As the American Society of Interior Designers (ASID) looked to launch its online community, Connex, it wanted technology that had some of the popular functionality of a decade-old bulletin board. "If I go on and see that you are on as well, I can page you," says Michael Alin, executive director. "That's always been incredibly popular with our members. I see who's there and I want to be there too."

Doing business across borders—geographic, industrial, disciplinary, even generational—reveals as many commonalities as differences. Our understanding of other mindsets, other ways of doing business informs and expands our own. The cross-pollination of ideas and the larger realm of networking contacts open us to previously unseen opportunities. But essentially, we seek like-minded individuals regardless of where they reside.

"In the UK, project management is a profession as well as a discipline," Langley says. "It has its own certification but it's something that other professions need to be trained in as well." Limiting membership to those who are project managers first rather than opening it to those who are, for instance, medical technicians who use project management skills not only lops off a huge opportunity for PMI but lessens the potential social capital available through membership.

ASID has only a few members outside the United States, most of them expatriates on assignment in other countries. Alin says it will be interesting to see whether that number grows based on the ability to network outside United States business hours.

REMAINING RELEVANT

There are more than thirty-two thousand Rotary clubs in more than two hundred countries and regions. It is a grassroots organization that seems local regardless of whether you're in Patagonia, Arizona, or Patagonia, Argentina.

Rotary clubs are "nonpolitical, nonreligious and open to all cultures, races and creeds," according to the Web site. Members join by invitation only.

Like many association members today, Rotary's members are aging. And because one must be invited to join, new members tend to look remarkably like current members. The average member is fifty-eight years old, slightly older than the typical association member in the United States. Such a member is, according to the William E. Smith Institute for Association Research, white, male, a college graduate, politically liberal, forty-six years of age, and living in a city.

Remaining relevant and attracting new, younger members is a major part of an initiative launched in 2005 by the Rotary Foundation. Future Vision is a "10-year vision with a three-year plan," says the Web site, based on extensive member research that showed aging members worldwide and declining membership in the United States. Changing demographics—the fear that the next generation of potential members will have other things on its mind and not be so interested in the sorts of activities in which their parents engaged—is a competitive threat not to be taken lightly. The book *Bowling Alone*, published in 2001, posits that Americans have become disconnected from existing communities, leading to less participation and increasing isolation.

Rotary's goal of eradicating polio is an important issue, but one with little resonance for younger potential members. Rotary's Future Vision plan, unveiled in mid 2008, includes six new global humanitarian issues. It devolves decision-making authority to local districts and councils, which are better able to court members at a grassroots level. And most importantly, it realizes that no association can be all things to all people but must put a stake in the ground that people can recognize and support.

The generations that grew up with technology and take for granted the ways in which it connects people are less interested in sitting in workshops or waiting for a research report. Information is becoming commoditized, and associations no longer can claim it as a competitive advantage. There are plenty of ways to find things out without paying dues. The Institute of Electrical and Electronics Engineers (IEEE), for instance, attracts members when they are engineering students with dues set at "less than a six-pack costs," says Jim Vick, publisher and editorial director of IEEE Media. "The problem is, we don't keep them. They get their community in other ways."

In 2006, the Smith Institute published a study called *Generations and the Future of Association Participation* that refutes the two main demographic fears for associations: that there are fewer people in Generation X and Generation Y than Baby Boomers, and that younger generations are less likely to join associations.

First, the population numbers are not that different, according to the study. Second, association membership is more a function of age than of generation. As people mature and reach higher earning potential, the likelihood of joining an association increases. Joining tends to happen in one's late thirties, according to the study, "when membership payoff begins to peak."

"Given rising incomes and improving job opportunities, today's young workers show every indication of joining associations at even higher rates than Baby Boomers, more than making up for their slightly smaller numbers." The study predicts that association membership will rise from about fifty-one million at present to about fifty-five million by the year 2015.

This seems like a great deal of wishful thinking. Associations apparently can sit on their hands and wait. They believe that when new generations become old enough, smart enough, and successful enough, they'll see the payoff and storm the membership offices. The fallacy is seeing the generational shift in isolation. The challenge to membership is not solely a function of age. While associations wait, the market is moving out from under them for reasons that are only partially due to changing demographics.

Demographic changes and technology go hand in hand in most association executives' minds. In particular, the ability to network online is seen as either a glass half full or half empty for associations.

"Most observers agree that associations can't create virtual communities," Benjamin Martin, CAE, director of communications and new media of the Virginia Association of REALTORS wrote in an article for ASAE. "Instead, such communities grow up from the grassroots."

While this seems incredibly shortsighted and vastly underestimates the ability of smart associations to utilize social media to their advantage, Martin says that the reverse is true. Associations overestimate their ability to create community online, he says, and don't allow them to develop organically.

American Business Media (ABM), the trade association for business-to-business publishers, launched its own social community in part as a membership acquisition tool. ABM members can invite nonmembers to join the community and, thus, see the benefits of membership. Groups will either survive or literally fall off the bottom of the page based on activity. Those that don't grow organically will wither and die.

Where associations can succeed at online community, according to Martin, is by devoting the resources at their disposal to cultivating the community. "There were four or five of us blogging a few years ago," he says, "but, very quickly, ASAE's Acronym blog had more subscribers than any of us because they had an organization behind it. They market it. They put it in their newsletter. It's a good object lesson for social networking sites."

Technology offers huge upside potential to associations, new ways of doing what they already do, as well as opportunities for entirely new products and services. ASID is spending almost 10 percent of its $13 million budget on technology. "We're in business to connect members to one another," ASID's Anil says. "The best connection ultimately is when members can talk to each other without our taking the lead all the time. A lot of times, our members are doing their ASID business at 2 a.m."

THE WORLD TILTS

In the last ten years, the biggest opportunity for business has been globalization. Almost half (42 percent) of ASAE's member organizations have members outside the United States, according to *Policies and Procedures in Association Management.* Individual member organizations are more likely than trade associations to attract members from overseas. Many of those members come almost by accident rather than recruitment. The IFT, based in Chicago, has twenty-two thousand members in more than eighty countries. But "no international members were recruited by us," says Barbara Byrd Keenan, CAE, IFT's executive vice president. "We never had a global strategy, no international outreach. Most of them came to us because they wanted to come to our annual meetings." The same is true of the Association of Collegiate Business Schools and Programs (ACBSP), according to its executive director, Doug Viehland, CAE. "They found us rather than us finding them," he says.

"Until 1997, we expressly had no international mission," says ASQ's Borawski. "Being a North American organization was part of our charter." Today ASQ has one hundred thousand members in 120 countries, 86 percent in North America, and focuses on four markets: China, India, Mexico, and Brazil. The group has hired an international marketing manager and has a wholly owned foreign enterprise (WOFE) in China.

ACBSP, IFT, and ASQ went into global markets carefully. They didn't lead with membership but rather relied on core strengths like content, accreditation, and education. When they look for members overseas, they try to get companies, not individuals, to join.

It is not difficult to understand why B2B associations increasingly are global. The search for revenue growth alone eventually would drive an ambitious association with a compelling value proposition outside its home market. B2B associations are going global for the same reason that B2B and B2C companies do: it's the way the world economy is moving.

Despite gloomy news about sub-prime mortgages, currency inequities, and a global economic recession, the global economy grew more than 4 percent for the fifth year in a row in 2007. Growth in the European Union was slightly higher than the United States. East Asia booked 10 percent growth and South Asia more than 8 percent. Eastern Europe was almost 7 percent and Africa, although plagued by chaos and war, rode commodity prices to more than 6 percent growth, according to the World Bank.

With this more or less even distribution, "The world's economic balance is tilting from rich industrialized countries to emerging markets," according to the January 26, 2008 edition of *The Economist*. Emerging economies now account for almost half of world output, and the International Monetary Fund predicts that for the first time this year China and India will be the largest contributors to worldwide growth. Those two countries, with their combined populations of 2.5 billion, are catching up with rich nations so quickly that the distinctions of First, Second, and Third World are becoming meaningless.

Globalization has fueled PMI's explosive growth. Even with 145 percent growth, 25 percent of it outside the United States, PMI's 260,000 members are a fraction of the potential of ten million project managers worldwide.

In the good old days when there were clear borders around things, associations were satisfied with the finite number of potential members. Associations weren't going to grow, but they also weren't going away. Member needs would change, but slowly, and doing the same thing in a new incarnation for the next generation of members could be sustained indefinitely. But all the walls are coming down—the Berlin Wall, the Great Wall, the firewall, the members-only wall. Associations have no borders; the flock is free to fly.

Questions

- Do online networks offer the same benefits as traditional associations?
- Could they if they wanted to?
- Will they ever replace associations?
- Can social capital be replicated online?

By the Numbers

- In the United States, there are 102,000 entities classified as membership organizations, according to the North American Industry Classification System codes from the U.S. Bureau of Labor Statistics. Most of them, 72,500, are B2B associations: trade and professional associations, business leagues, and chambers of commerce.
- In the Philippines, there are more than 60,000 associations registered with the Securities and Exchange Commission.
- In China, of the estimated 153,000 registered Social Organizations, fewer than 2,000 operate at a national level.
- In the UK, there are more than 8,000 associations.
- In Australia, associations spend between A$27 billion and A$43 billion annually.
- More than 50 percent of all international association business now occurs in Europe, according to ASAE.

The Case for Membership

The American Planning Association (APA) is ninety-one years old and has nearly forty thousand members. Membership is open to anyone, not only working, degreed city planners. The largest part of APA's revenue stream is from membership dues; the APA is very good at up-selling within the membership.

Planners with a few years of experience are allowed to take a certification exam and become members of the American Institute of Certified Planners (AICP), a division of the APA. Members of AICP pay extra dues and must continue to pay those dues in order to retain certification. About half of the professional city planners who are members of APA are also members of AICP. Retention for APA has topped 80 percent for the last ten years, 90 percent for AICP.

APA recently added so-called certification maintenance—as in, continuing education units—to AICP membership. Certification maintenance was offered for the first time at the 2008 annual conference, where attendance was higher than ever.

APA also has about twenty special interest groups whose members pay extra dues as well. Each group has its own e-newsletter, most of them hosted by APA.

To attract students, APA approached the eighty or so accredited university programs in the United States. Most of those shared their student databases with APA. Students can join the association for free in their first year, and there is a nominal payment in the second year. Further, for the first few years after graduation, there is a New Professionals rate. Student members and new professionals have special programming at conferences and separate receptions at meetings. They receive the *New Planners* e-newsletter and can post their resumes to the job board where entry-level jobs are listed.

APA launched a growth strategy in 2003 with the goal of increasing membership by fifteen thousand in ten years. At the time of writing, this plan is ahead of schedule. APA leaders feel that, even though several nonmember publications are offered, member dollars are a more reliable growth area.

The Case for Non-Membership

Membership dues account for less than one-third of total revenues at the 156-year-old American Society of Civil Engineers (ASCE), and the figure is approaching one-quarter. "I think that's good," says Pat Natale, CAE and executive director of the group. "It's a matter of growing other things, serving needs, coming up with new things and trying them out."

The 140,000-member association has annual revenues of $54 million, $20 million of that from publications. There are fifteen hundred books and thirty journals in the catalog, all peer-reviewed. The Civil Engineering Database contains more than one hundred thousand bibliographic and abstract records of everything ASCE has published since 1970. *Civil Engineering* magazine is published monthly. The full set of contract documents available for sale numbers twenty-one, a few of which are available for free download.

ASCE's eight institutes are open to non–civil engineers and attract such professionals as environmental lawyers, for instance, or architects, geologists, and transportation engineers. Each institute has a shelf-load of publications of its own. In foreign markets, ASCE leads with its publications, and membership is secondary. There are multiple memoranda of understanding in place with similar organizations outside the United States, a partnership model that Natale sees increasingly used both domestically and internationally.

There also is a heavy emphasis on developing new products and services. One of the things that Natale brought to his association career after twenty-eight years as a utility company executive is a culture of entrepreneurship. "You have to reward the try," he says. "We've been doing that a lot here, celebrating attempts. We don't nurture things forever. We kill it if it doesn't work but nurture the entrepreneurial spirit."

ASCE is launching a building security standard similar to LEED (Leadership in Energy and Environmental Design) as part of its new Infrastructure Security Partnership. It is developing new manuals to improve the design process of civil engineering projects, and it convened a group in 2008 to try to envision what the engineering profession will look like in twenty years.

"Associations must move from the sense of just being service-oriented," Natale says, "which is very important, but they must maintain a level of profitability. Change your business model. Change your systems."

Chapter 2

The Nature of an Association

All happy families are happy in the same way.

—Leo Tolstoy

The first association you ever joined probably was analogous to the Girl Scouts, with or without the uniforms. The nature of all associations, B2C and B2B alike, is essentially the same. They offer a community of like-minded souls that will welcome you with meetings large and small. They also offer education of some sort, advocacy on member's behalf (the Girl Scouts' fifty-six-year-old advocacy office lobbies for the prevention of youth violence, among other things), research for and about their members, and regular communications (*Boys Life* magazine has been published by the Boy Scouts since 1911). B2B associations often are the standards-setting bodies for their industries or professions, but that is the only substantial grown-up difference.

Before technological tools provided a substitute, most associations (like all political bodies), were local and based on face-to-face interaction. International associations—the Freemasons, founded in the 1600s, is the oldest—are mostly federations, which is the nearly universal model of associations in Europe. The Belgian XYZ Association is its country's representative in the European XYZ Federation—a domestic association connected to other domestic associations.

Globalization and technology eliminate the borders but do not change association core competencies. Nearly half of an association's budget goes to three activities: education, convention planning and meeting activities, and lobbying, according to *Associations Matter: Associations by the Numbers*. In most cases, another significant chunk of money goes to some form of research, and the final piece is earmarked for communication.

Globalization and technology do, however, significantly alter the nature of associations. The interaction is not necessarily face-to-face, the delivery no longer may be personal, and lines of communication are simultaneously very long and incredibly short. The world is smaller, and the horizon a lot closer.

A domestic membership-based organization becomes a research provider abroad, a credentialing body, a source of education, and a standards setter. The membership model gives way to what the new market actually needs. "Individuals are increasingly moving away from being 'members' to be being 'buyers' of products, services, offerings, benefits or access to networks and communities," says Thomas Reiser, director of the International Society of Nephrology (ISN) and MCI healthcare practice leader. "Associations' focus should not necessarily be on how to retain members or recruit them, but what it can do to make itself and its products/services/offerings/benefits truly relevant to the 'customers'/potential members."

It is why some foreign members renew year after year, even with no possibility for face-to-face interaction. Perhaps this is why so many members in general, the checkbook members, renew but never attend. They donate to a cause they support in return for a magazine or some other tangible and hopefully valuable benefit that doesn't ask them to do anything. "What really matters," Reiser says, "is not necessarily how many paying members an organization has, but how many 'customers/contacts/friends' it can a) reach, b) influence and c) ideally involve in its network/community."

This makes *unbundling* both simpler and more complicated. On one hand, the association now can exploit one or more of its core competencies without the pressure of establishing a full-blown clone of itself outside its borders. On the other hand, knowing exactly what people want and delivering it without the constant feedback loop of membership participation means embarking on market research in unfamiliar terrain—a different country, a different age group, or a different part of the value chain.

Internally, the problem is that the entire infrastructure is built to support the membership model. It's what associations know and understand, and reorganizing to support new models that must coexist is painful, messy, and largely resisted.

Operations become much more complex even as the core remains the same. The type and level of education may be lower, more basic than in the association's backyard. Or it could be higher. Meetings may be far away, with all the complications of remote planning and execution, or virtual, or with avatars (see Chapter 3). Research now means more statistics and different trends, often with data that does not match the existing, long-established categories. Publications must be mailed, at great expense, to overseas members—although digital versions can lower costs—and decisions must be made about whether or not to translate and, if so, into what languages. And although advocacy for the industry or the profession still matters, direct political lobbying may no longer be appropriate.

The association has to become more innovative, develop more and better products and services. But delivering those products and services stretches an already stretched organization. Associations are always understaffed—always. But often, they have too much of what they don't need—outdated processes and operations that could be more efficiently outsourced—and not enough of what they do need—cutting-edge technology and market trend expertise.

The *organizational structure* must become somewhat schizophrenic. A mature enterprise in the headquarters country must work with an entrepreneurial operation overseas. The former usually moves slowly and may rule its competitive landscape. The latter moves quickly, adjusting to competitive pressures on the fly. The person or committee that "owns" the globalization effort will in most ways be truly "foreign" and, given the travel necessary, seldom seen. The person that owns young-member recruitment may seem, in his or her way, equally foreign—i.e., younger. And the technology people will speak in a seemingly foreign tongue of made-up-sounding words and acronyms.

"[This schizophrenia] taxes the association culture and is difficult to manage," says Robin Lokerman, CEO of association management company MCI.

And, most frightening and transformative of all, the *business model* changes entirely. The membership model implodes. Chopping up an association into individual products, going for reach and influence rather than dues, dramatically changes the financial proposition. Each product must recoup its costs with a healthy margin in the face of stiff competition among audiences that may never have heard of the group.

"Our print revenue is going to hell in a handbasket," says Jim Vick, publisher of IEEE Media, "and I don't have the options that a commercial publisher has. We have to publish the same folio size [page count] in Europe, Asia and Latin America regardless of whether we can get ad support. All that has to be subsidized."

The burden on each product and service to perform has never been higher, and the comforting safety net of the large institutional operating budget disappears.

In other words, what the association *does* has not changed. *How* it does it—how it manages it and how it gets paid—must change completely.

THE SEARCH FOR RELEVANCE

Nearly half of American associations have members outside the United States. That percentage has remained constant since 1995, but between 2001 and 2005 (the date of the most recent study), there have been increases in both the number of members and member participation in associations, according to ASAE's *Policies and Procedures in Association Management.*

For more than half of those American associations with members outside the United States, international members pay the same dues as domestic members. The vast majority, 86 percent, also receive the same membership services and products. This does not mean, however, that they receive country- or region-specific services and products. Rather, they receive the same magazine, the same discounts on conferences, and the same educational opportunities as anyone else, any or all of which may not be relevant to their specific circumstances.

Associations are not alone in this. "One 2005 study found that less than half of the *Forbes 900* firms who target international customers actually bothered to create any kind of a tailored experience for them," according to C. David Gammel, president of High Context Consulting and author of the longest-running association blog (www.highcontext.com/weblog).

The same could be said for younger members. Associations seem to think that doing the same things—but online—will automatically appeal to the supposedly more tech-savvy group. They try to remain relevant by balancing on these two flawed assumptions: one, that what they do is relevant to the new audience, and two, that young people are more tech-savvy just because they're younger. In the absence of research that proves either thing, shoveling existing products online is a wasted exercise.

Many associations are just at the point of deciding to go global rather than simply accept the dues of international members. They are becoming proactive in their globalization efforts, attaching return-on-investment (ROI) projections to the strategic plan and wading through the operational challenges. They are grappling with the unbundling necessary to enter new markets, which demands the Herculean effort of shedding the "we've always done it that way" mindset.

In the process, they are learning that global expansion is not simply about a search for new revenues. It is a transformative process that demands hard choices and long-term commitment from both the board and the staff. Going global takes the organization full circle, however. It drives mindful associations back to the value proposition so that, instead of trying to protect outmoded processes, they reconnect with the implications of delivering their brand promise.

The same process will enable associations to unlock the value proposition for new generations of members. Analyzing that market in much the same way as a foreign one—which it is in many ways—will force a reexamination of what the organization stands for and how it fulfills that mission. Finding ways to do that in a valuable, meaningful manner only demands hard work and an open mind.

"Whatever ASQ [the American Society for Quality] can do to advance the cause of quality, that makes economic sense, we desire to do," says Paul Borawski, ASQ executive director and chief strategist. "Is it about growth? Yes, but not about domination. We are responding to the signals of need in a world growing in its interest of quality."

According to *7 Measures of Success: What Remarkable Associations Do that Others Don't*, exceptionally successful associations continuously gather and analyze data and make decisions based on their analysis. They scan the external environment while conducting ongoing internal market research. "This requires a willingness to ask, 'What do we now know, and what are we going to do about it,'" according to the study.

"Use field research to discover latent needs," says Jeneanne Rae, president of Alexandria, Virginia-based Peer Insight LLC, a service innovation consortium. "Continue to use surveys that get to the explicit top-of-mind needs."

The Society for Human Resource Management (SHRM), for instance, pursues an annual process it calls "purposeful abandonment" by which it cleans its closets of underperforming products, services, and management techniques. "Changing the way you do things is a process not a policy," says Gary Rubin, chief publishing and e-media officer/group publisher. "Staying close to your readers/members, having a mechanism to actively reach out for information to understand what the needs drivers for these people are—you've got to be in the market. A blind horse can't win a race."

As associations confront the myriad challenges and opportunities—from globalization to changing demographics, from technological change to consolidation—their main objective is to remain relevant. That is the constant around which everything else has moved. "What's our global identity?" asks Vick at IEEE Media. "What's our relevance?"

GLOBAL TRAJECTORY

The trajectory from domestic to global is typically three steps:

1. International by default (i.e., provide what you can)

2. International by design (i.e., provide different products for overseas markets)

3. Global (i.e., respond market-by-market)

Put another way, according to Lokerman, a U.S. association moves to a most-favored-nation model, adding Canada, for instance. This leads to a regional model—the regions that make the most sense rather than country-by-country. This is followed by an international model with multiple locations and a heavy use of electronic communication. Finally comes the fully global model with global leadership and staff structure. Virtual presence may substitute for some of the expensive brick-and-mortar presence that the trajectory traditionally included.

And that shows that the same trajectory can be used for entering any new market:

1. Give them what they want when you can

2. Provide different products in different markets

3. Give them what they want, when they want it, and the way they want it

This, of course, demands new skills and a different set of infrastructure investments. Associations that make a conscious decision to pursue this trajectory must gather both external and internal data. They unlock the logjam on decision making that traditionally slows associations. They gain a thorough understanding of their industry or discipline, their competitors, and their members, enabling them to make better decisions and adjust to changes. But they also gain internal consensus, which makes them nimbler and more responsive to the competitive environment.

"In associations, knowledge drives trust and trust drives nimbleness," Glenn Tucker and colleagues say in *The Will to Govern Well*. "If vision is clear and values are shared and lived, the activities chosen by the association today or tomorrow will be the best ones it can find at the time to fulfill the vision. The activities themselves should not become the point; rather, their purpose is progress toward the vision."

With a complete top-to-bottom understanding of their missions, associations know what can be changed without compromising those missions. And because they continuously track data, they know whether a change is achieving the necessary results. This enables the association to shed outdated practices rather than bog down with the status quo. Great associations also build successful alliances, according to the *7 Steps to Success* study, which is a key to entering global markets.

"We will not go international without a partner," says Peter J. O'Neil, assistant executive director of the American Industrial Hygiene Association (AIHA). AIHA is extremely confident about what it does well, but recognizes the holes in its abilities and the need for external partners. The twelve-thousand-member association is ruthless in walking away from partnerships that don't live up to expectations.

What associations do in this new competitive environment is what they've always done. How they deliver it, what they charge for it, and the returns they reap are drastically different. The terror of becoming irrelevant is well-placed, but globalization is proving that the world wants what associations have to sell. Associations need to unlock their products and services and become user-centric instead of institution-centric. They are behind for-profits in going global, but that only means that associations have plenty of examples of success and failure from which to learn.

RESEARCH

Of the core competencies of a B2B association, research is a major asset. Large, well-organized for-profit organizations, however, increasingly are eating into association research business. "Associations don't have the deep pockets and IT scale of billion-dollar research companies and publishers to create extensive data- or news-gathering operations," according to the *Future of the Competitive Association* study. "They lack the editorial freedom to sell incisive, no-holds-barred research or news on the state of individual member companies."

That is still true, but trade associations especially can create extremely valuable research that no for-profit company can provide. Associations leverage their relationships with members into data that is unavailable anywhere else. For example, the Metals Service Center Institute (MSCI) provides the Metals Activity Report—providing data on shipments and inventories from its members to its members—which is an indicator proven more useful from a strategic planning perspective than ever-changing metals commodities prices.

"We get paid in two ways," says Chris Marti, MSCI director of research. "Companies participate; I consider that a form of payment. There are very valuable benefits that accrue to the organization as more companies participate. That elbow grease is critical to the association. The value proposition built into our research products is that members who participate get a lot of information that no one else gets. Second, there are hard dollars in two different revenue streams: subscriptions to the data (non-members) and companies that join because of the data. The hard dollars alone are about at the level of funding the report."

Without the membership relationship, global research or country-by-country international research is that much harder. The trust necessary to share data does not exist, and there is no proprietary mechanism for disseminating it in a useful way. "We have the dues that are at least enough to fund the start-up," Marti says. "For-profit researchers don't have that." MSCI's research is outsourced to a trusted third party so there is no chance that anything will leak via a staff member. Most of the members are privately held companies so the information would never be available publicly and there is no way for anyone else to replicate it.

Research is, however, the most inherently global undertaking of an association. Looking at data in the largest possible context adds a new dimension that is both informative and marketable. People are always interested in knowing where they stand, both close to home and in the larger world. Members will always want the competitive advantage of early warning on trends; it is one of the major benefits of membership. For example, MSCI member companies like Goldman Sachs receive the Metals Activity Report twenty-four hours in advance of general distribution, which is a huge advantage for them.

ADVOCACY

Associations don't make money on advocacy. The idea is that the members will make money based on the association's advocacy efforts; either legislation will be more favorable or the profession will be enhanced. The payoff for the association is in attracting and retaining members.

As associations change and the membership model becomes less pervasive, advocacy must be undertaken like recruiting efforts for a political campaign, rallying people around a cause. "Some associations will impose a special dues assessment to help them deal with an unbudgeted but important issue," says Doug Pinkham, president of the Public Affairs Council. "Sometimes members can elect to take part in a special coalition and then combine their resources to fund that campaign."

Advocacy is not easily translated to the global arena, particularly in the form of direct political lobbying. Political clout takes volume, a number of members worth paying attention to. Influencing legislation is a country-by-country endeavor and, although some associations are developing global advocacy platforms, the cost may be far too high for the results. "The challenge—for both a company and an association—is maintaining a common set of principles and messages when you are working in different political systems and cultures," Pinkham says.

Trade associations with corporate members who are themselves global have a jump start on gaining an audience and conveying a credible message. Professional associations whose members work for global corporations share some of that potential. But a largely U.S.-based association sending representatives to the European Union will need more grassroots support to have its message heard.

"It's not lobbying in the traditional sense," Pinkham says. "It's an integrated approach that uses a host of strategies such as media relations and public awareness programs to weigh in on public opinion."

Associations also must guard against the assumption that issues, trends, and best practices in one country instantly translate to another. The urge to be condescending is driven as much by cost as by naiveté. "Given America's poor reputation around the world, global associations based in the U.S. need to be careful that they are not perceived as being heavy-handed in their advocacy," Pinkham says. "It's vital to spend a lot of time listening to other points of view and truly understanding everyone else's position on an issue."

Two advocacy trends that work well in the global market are an integrated approach to political communication and the use of coalitions for special, targeted initiatives.

In 2002, a coalition of U.S.-based associations worked with large chemical companies to modify the European Union's REACH plan (Registration, Evaluation and Authorization of Chemicals). An analysis by the American Chemistry Council (ACC) was used by the Bush Administration, with input from the Synthetic Organic Chemical Manufacturers Association, the American Plastics Council, and the Chemical Industrial Sector Advisory Committee. "These efforts helped to build an aggressive position worldwide, and brought about significant concessions in the draft now being considered by the European parliament," claimed ACC's 2003 annual report.

According to the 2007 ASAE report *The Decision to Join*, government advocacy ranks lower in importance to international members, but public advocacy is equal to or higher than among domestic members. International members may not be entirely comfortable with political lobbying by a nondomestic association, "but they are concerned about the reputation of their company or their industry around the world," Pinkham says. "They think it is desirable for the association to play a major role in ensuring that this reputation remains or become positive."

In China, there is a growing focus on corporate social responsibility and associations with a strong CSR advocacy stance "go to the front of the queue," says Rohit Talwar, futurist and CEO of the London, U.K.-based think tank

Fast Future Ventures. In this instance, international constituencies "naturally are thinking more about public advocacy than government advocacy," Pinkham says.

Advocacy, regardless of the type, is a minefield of regulatory, cultural, sociological, and political intricacies. "It's hard to imagine an association doing this on a global scale on its own without a lot of in-country expertise," Pinkham says. "If the association's members are large multinationals, that expertise may reside within the group. But in the majority of cases these associations would be wise to hire well-regarded consultants to assist them."

MEETINGS

A 2008 IMEX Research study on association meeting trends found that although associations were placing tighter controls on event costs, they also were working to attract participation from "less rich" emerging countries, often by subsidizing their attendance. According to the study, associations value multiculturalism and, in some cases, make it their highest priority in meeting planning.

The American Society for Therapeutic Radiology and Oncology offers a huge variety of travel grants for events; most are one thousand dollars each or fifteen hundred dollars for international travel. Some associations, especially in healthcare, include registration at the annual conference in membership dues. The lower dues paid by those outside the United States is a form of subsidy for all programming.

The problem with subsidized conference participation is, of course, the financial model. The same expenses are incurred—speakers, meals, meeting rooms, materials, etc.—but the revenues per participant have fallen. The meeting looks extremely successful from an attendance standpoint but may not be making as much money. The balance between profitability and longer-term strategic goals can be difficult to find, especially with such a traditional cash cow as meetings.

The need for profitability can be married to the need for relevance, however, to the benefit of both.

"Large international conferences are evolving into smaller, more focused conferences, which sometimes take place in a specific region only," says Michael Podt, conference manager of MCI Brussels. As long as certain costs can be amortized across these smaller regional meetings and other costs lowered because of the tighter focus, meetings can achieve both hard and soft ROI.

The IMEX study also found that a trend toward electronic meetings was being met with considerable skepticism given the "importance of personal chemistry at meetings" and the difficulty of getting online participants to pay. This is, however, not the experience of for-profit meeting planners. Unisfair, a virtual meeting platform, will be used by 225 for-profit meetings in 2008. Attendance at eComXpo, a virtual tradeshow for ecommerce marketers, runs between 5,000 and 8,000. The reluctance, therefore, lies with associations rather than with potential attendees. Of the three main reasons to attend a conference—to learn, to network, and to visit an exotic location—electronic meetings compete very well on two of the three.

On the exotic location front, some associations are very exotic indeed. The Professional Photographers of America organizes a cruise off the coast of New England in the fall. Along with the enhanced staterooms, an ice rink, and a spa, the ship provides views of the fall foliage along the North Atlantic coastline, and the association provides professional photography classes.

According to *The Decision to Join*, networking is much more important to foreign members than domestic ones, and they are more likely to be what the study calls "ad hoc volunteers." They tend not to serve on committees—distance also weighs against that—but to speak at events and contribute or review content. Training and development rank higher in importance among domestic members, but that is largely due to distance and may well be overcome as distance learning vehicles catch up.

ASSOCIATION PUBLISHING

According to a 2006 survey by *Folio* magazine, 59 percent of association respondents in the United States have global membership, and most still rely on print magazines as their primary communication vehicle.

At the 2008 ASAE International Conference, one of the most striking omissions was any mention of association publications as a part of global outreach. And yet, many associations lead with content as a way to enter new markets.

The American Industrial Hygiene Association has international site license agreements for publications. PMI has an extensive translation network for its books, and the *Project Management Body of Knowledge* (PMBOK), the study of which is necessary to the credentials exam, is translated into eight languages. IEEE has a literature library called IEL containing 1.6 million documents, which China licenses for academics. "Dues are a fraction of our membership," says Jim Vick, IEEE publisher and editorial director. "We're a massive information machine. We make our money that way."

In China, the Chinese Institute of Food Science and Technology (CIFST) repurposes content by publishing the (U.S.) Institute of Food Technologists (IFT) flagship magazine, *Food Technology*. Of the content, 80 percent comes from IFT and the other 20 percent from CIFST. The Chinese organization handles all translation, production, and distribution. "Because we already have the content in the magazine, there is very little expense to us," says IFT Executive Vice President Barbara Byrd Keenan. "They [CIFST] bear the expense."

IFT expects the jointly published magazine to make a profit within the next three years based on outside support and the fee that CIFST pays for licensing. The content eventually will be available online in China, and IFT has the right to use the translated content on its own site.

Using content to lead an association's expansion into a new international market accomplishes several things:

- It is inexpensive, since existing content can be repurposed and it can be published online to avoid the expense of print and international postage. The only new cost is translation.

- It is measurable, especially in an online medium, and so can test the waters for future programming.

- It quickly establishes credibility in a market where the association has no reputation or track record.

- It is the surest, most consistent way to extend a brand, since exposure to an association's content is many members' only interaction with the brand. Not only do members and potential members gain information, they see what the brand promise consists of and how the association fulfills that promise.

In the new association world of competition and eroding membership, the publishing program is potentially a huge source of revenue. The Society for Human Resource Management (SHRM) earns $28 million in publishing revenues annually. With a membership of almost a quarter of a million, it can charge top dollar for advertising and sponsorships both in print and online as long as it backs it up with very high-quality products.

"Diversifying revenue streams is critical for any business," Gary Rubin, SHRM chief publishing officer, says. "Any business leader that only has one product to sell should be worried. It's classic marketing. Associations think what they sell is membership. That's like the Pony Express thinking it was in the business of horses and paper rather than in the delivery business. Association executives that see their business as selling membership rather than creating value for a community through a variety of things—conferences, collaboration, publications, etc. I think they're missing their reason for being."

STANDARDS AND CREDENTIALS

One of the best, surest, most desirable ways to enter new markets is through standards and credentials. Standards are a huge potential revenue source. Only 7.4 percent of the members of the American Society of Mechanical Engineers (ASME) are outside the United States, but 40 percent of codes and standards are sold overseas. Some 40 percent of the AIHA's revenues come from its accreditation of laboratories.

IFT's joint publishing endeavor not only allows it to "lead with our signature strengths: education and content," Keenan says, but to gain an endorsement as the global standards body for food safety. There are many organizations similar to IFT in Europe, but European Union food safety standards are very different from those in the United States. "China would be a very potent ally vis-à-vis Europe," Keenan says.

Credentials are another extremely desirable association product. Much of the Project Management Institute's spectacular growth has been based on its credential, the Project Management Professional, or PMP. The PMP's career enhancement for individuals and the shared business methods for companies make for a powerful combination. PMI also is aggressively developing new standards and certifications. "Six years ago, we had one standard," says Mark Langley, executive vice president and chief operating officer. "Today we have thirteen."

As ASQ moved into four overseas markets, it has led with certification. "The China Association for Quality wants our logo on the certification," Borowski says.

Gary Boyler, executive director of the International Coach Federation, says, "If your credentialing is global, you can practice anywhere in the world. It becomes a career advancement tool for the credential holder. As corporations hire their own coaches, credentialing is preferred if not required."

Boyler's board, with six European members, has approved a move to International Organization for Standardization (ISO) compliance. "It's a great line in the sand for us in terms of being global," he says. "We're building a body of knowledge with a learning domain. The role delineation study is almost complete. The testing portion will be given in a proctored and secure environment with another portion, as you get to higher credentials, where we'll tape an actual coaching session and have that critiqued. It's the hybrid of knowledge and competency."

The ISO compliance program will take two years to complete and will lead to three levels of credentialing: associate, professional, and master.

"It fulfills our mission," Boyler says. "It's also a revenue generation and membership retention tool. No doubt about it."

"Our most successful activities in China are our certification programs and our standards activities," says Kim Sterling, CAE and vice president of marketing for IPC, the Association Connecting Electronics Industries. "We have Chinese engineers involved in reviewing, translating, and commenting on IPC standards. The revenues are very important, but the standards are also the foundation of other programs. We have a thriving certification program based on our five most widely used standards. Also, our members have identified our standards as the most important benefit of membership."

GOVERNANCE

Every association has a board of directors. The tripartite structure of board-staff-members is central to the nature of associations. In the future, this structure itself will not change, but the capabilities of the board and the staff must change to adequately out-compete the competition (see Chapter 6).

Although conventional wisdom says that the board is strategic and the staff is tactical, boards often are not capable of being strategic enough, of seeing the future and acting on it rather than reacting when finally backed into a corner. "The board has got to be out there into the future," says Pat Natale, CAE, executive director of the American Society of Civil Engineers, and incoming president of the Council of Engineering and Scientific Society Executives. "They have to be visionary." Board membership will have to be based on something more than tenure or filling an arbitrary category like region or industry vertical.

Staffs need to be more concerned with strategic execution than tactics. Skill level and expertise needs to be "extraordinary," Rubin says. "Some organizations may have people who are not prepared, or don't want, to be extraordinary. They just want jobs."

Board meetings also must change: more efficient, more focused, more willing to deal with complex issues in productive ways rather than simple consensus.

In short, the governance structure of associations will have to lead. Leadership is much more difficult than management—the day-to-day, more or less forward momentum that can be as much inertia as direction. Leadership will be the difference between where associations are and where they need to be in the new competitive landscape.

By the Numbers

- 42% of associations polled by ASAE in the United States have members located outside the United States.

- 18.4% of associations' operating budgets are devoted to member education programs.

  o 17% goes to convention planning and meeting activities.

  o 13.5% is budgeted for lobbying.

  o 4.9% is allocated to advocacy communications (print, radio, and TV advertising).

- The average association spends $509,000 on publication-related products and services.

- 26% spend $1 million or more.

- 48% of association magazines and journals generate a net profit after direct expenses and salary.

- The median profit on advertising sales of $1.6 million is $420,139.

- Most associations publish monthly.

- 22% publish five to nine separate publications.

- 22% publish three publications.

- The average is eight publications per association (print and electronic, combined).

- 90% of associations produce a magazine.

- 78% produce an e-newsletter.

- 45% produce a print newsletter.

- 34% produce a scholarly journal.

- 15% produce newspapers and tabloids.

- 56% of association magazines are produced by professional associations; 29% by trade associations.

- 22% claim that 10% to 24% of association revenue comes from publications.

- 20% claim 1% to 9% of association revenue comes from publications.
- The average association brings in $6.5 million annually.
- 91% of total revenue comes from print; 68% from advertising, 23% from subscriptions.
- 6% of revenue comes from online and e-media ventures.

How to Go Global

1. Compensate for your weaknesses by forming strategic partnerships with complementary organizations.

2. Understand why you are going global. Without clear objectives, you won't know whether you're succeeding or failing.

3. Choose locations in terms of what will work for your value proposition and your programming offerings.

4. Know what you can handle operationally, and tailor your expectations to those capabilities.

5. Accept that you'll make mistakes. Be ready to learn from them, adjust quickly, and move on.

6. Be humble rather than chauvinistic, and know that you have much to learn from foreign members.

Questions

The *Generations and the Future of Association Participation* study by the William E. Smith Institute for Association Research asks:

- What kinds of returns do younger people seek and demand in return for membership?

    Based on largely anecdotal data, the study predicts that younger members tend to demand higher levels of accountability, identifiable career advantages, and opportunities to serve within the association.

Other questions:

- What will nondomestic members want from an association membership?
- What are their needs?
- What are the differences in their ecosystem?
- What demands will they make on membership ROI?
- Will they behave differently in terms of involvement and renewal?

Speak to Me

In a study by Common Sense Advisory, a translation consultancy, most large, for-profit companies in fifteen globally dominant countries offer Web sites in two languages, their home-country language and one other. Although the firm advocates global companies doing everything in-language by country of operation, the study admits that such an ambition is an "ideal world" goal and that the expense and complexity involved would be prohibitive.

Instead, the study uncovered the twenty-five countries where the gross domestic product accounts for more than 80 percent of the world's economy and the ten "mega-languages" that account for three-quarters of the people on the Web.

"You can achieve maximum return by localizing your way through these top 25 economies," according to the study. Further, "if your goal is to maximize brand awareness, you can get the maximum bang for your buck by limiting your Web outreach to just 10 languages."

10 MEGA-LANGUAGES

	% of Total Online Population
English	26.9
Simplified Chinese	14.2
Japanese	7.4
Spanish	7.3
German	4.9
Portuguese	4.0
French	3.5
Korean	2.9
Italian	2.7
Russian	2.4

TOP 25 COUNTRIES BY GDP

2007 Rank	Country	GDP* in US$ (billions)	% of 2007 GWP	% of GWP** Cumulative	Internet Users (millions)	Dominant Language >60%
1	United States	13,244.5	27.0	27.0	205.3	English
2	Japan	4,367.4	8.9	35.9	86.3	Japanese
3	Germany	2,897.0	5.9	41.8	50.6	German
4	China	2,630.1	5.4	47.1	123.0	Chinese
5	United Kingdom	2,374.6	4.8	52.0	37.6	English
6	France	2,231.6	4.5	56.5	29.9	French
7	Italy	1,852.5	3.8	60.3	28.8	Italian
8	Canada	1,269.0	2.6	62.9	21.9	English/French
9	Spain	1,225.7	2.5	65.3	19.2	Spanish
10	Brazil	1,067.7	2.2	67.5	25.9	Portuguese
11	Russia	979.0	2.0	69.5	23.7	Russian
12	South Korea	888.2	1.8	71.3	33.9	Korean
13	India	886.8	1.8	73.1	60.0	English/Hindi
14	Mexico	840.0	1.7	74.8	18.6	Spanish
15	Australia	754.8	1.5	76.4	14.6	English
16	Netherlands	663.1	1.4	77.7	10.8	Dutch
17	Belgium	393.5	0.8	78.5	5.1	Dutch/French
18	Turkey	392.4	0.8	79.3	16.0	Turkish
19	Sweden	385.2	0.8	80.1	6.8	Swedish
20	Switzerland	377.2	0.8	80.9	5.0	German
21	Indonesia	364.2	0.7	81.6	16.0	Indonesian
22	Taiwan	355.7	0.7	82.3	13.2	Chinese
23	Saudi Arabia	348.6	0.7	83.1	3.2	Arabic
24	Poland	338.6	0.7	83.7	10.6	Polish
25	Norway	335.2	0.7	84.4	3.1	Norwegian

*Gross Domestic Product
**Gross World Product

Chapter 3

Online Community

Only connect.

—E. M. Forster

I'm in Minneapolis visiting my son. One of my best friends from when I lived in Greece now lives in Australia. I've just e-mailed her an article from the *New York Times* about Andorra la Vella, the tiny tax haven where she lived for five years. Along with the article, I included photos of my now-grown children, a music clip from The World's Most Dangerous Polka Band, and congratulatory best wishes on her fortieth wedding anniversary. It's tomorrow and autumn in her rain-forest home; I'm enduring the American Midwest's snowy version of spring. She now has a rich, multimedia communication that will make her feel like she was a part of my weekend and I was a part of hers.

When I met this friend in the mid 1970s, this little spur-of-the-moment communiqué would have taken three weeks to arrive—probably longer while I got the pictures developed. Our friendship has survived all these years on three continents in three countries on my part and six on hers, all via Christmas cards, telex, fax, snail mail, and now e-mail. Obviously things are a lot easier now, and today's communications make this feel more like friendship than random missives to someone on the other side of the world.

Would this work if I never had known her personally? Would I communicate this way with someone I'd never met? Even with all the rich media in the world, would the connection exist?

WHAT IS WHAT

First, some definitions. Digital media is evolving at a thousand miles per hour with its hair on fire. Even those of us who work in media companies struggle to keep up. Unless you're online all the time and truly live and breathe the technology and its applications, you will inevitably go to a meeting and hear made-up, oddly spelled words (Twitter, Flickr, Digg) whose meaning you cannot even guess.

Terms for overarching concepts often are used interchangeably, adding to the confusion. Rich media, social media, online community, social networks, interactivity, virtual reality—the meaning depends on the context and, even then, is often fuzzy. The writer and/or speaker may be equally fuzzy about it, and the confusion mounts.

For the purposes of this book, the meanings are as follows:

- **Interactive Media:** The initial interactive tools that the Web allowed: Listservs, forums, chat, bulletin boards, and real-time polls and charts. This is not the same thing as *interactivity*—that's something the user does; interactive media is something that allows, even invites, interactivity to happen.

- **Web 2.0:** The point at which we move from a read-only Web to a read-write Web.

- **Rich Media:** The applications that go beyond static text—the advance edge of Web 2.0: blogs, podcasts, streaming audio and video, digital magazines, webcasts, webinars, and the like.

- **Social Media:** Another name for online community. True communities that ask you to join, invite friends, and interact with them in an open environment. Social media involves real-time communication with other people.

Each of these overlaps the others. Except for social media, all well-built Web sites these days employ as many of these applications as are appropriate to the subject matter and the audience. The goal is engagement.

- **Engagement:** The point beyond stickiness—the point at which a user is loyal. This includes people who "lurk," i.e., never interact, but who come back again and again because they find the content valuable and the applications useful.

To play on the famous phrase about possessions: have nothing on your site that you do not know to be useful or feel to be relevant, and you will likely create engagement.

RICHER AND RICHER

The pull of rich media is obvious. According to Nielsen's VideoCensus, more than 116 million users watched online video clips in January 2008, which translates to more than 5.9 billion video downloads. They watched for an average of more than 120 minutes and downloaded more than fifty streams per person.

Interactive media remain extremely popular and an integral part of many association's online offerings. Electronic mailing lists or discussion groups (such as Listservs) often are "the most visible member benefit," says Andy Steggles, chief information officer of the Risk and Insurance Management Society (RIMS), and one that allows member-to-member networking. New Listserv technology goes well beyond the ugly formats and limited functionality of the old. Branding, sponsorship, attachments, and integration into a resource library are all now possible, greatly enhancing the value of something members long ago embraced.

When you add social media, the stampede to digital engagement is even more compelling. Of U.S. Internet users, 66 percent visited a social-media site in January 2008, according to comScore Media Metrix, and Forrester Research predicts that spending on social media will increase 150 percent in 2008 over the previous year.

"I know of 15 associations that are launching social networks this year," Steggles says. "Associations have to do this, they have no choice."

By 2009, social networks will be ubiquitous. Smaller and/or regional associations are creating a presence on Facebook and LinkedIn where their members already gather. "At this point, Facebook has 60 million or 70 million subscribers," says Ben Martin, director of communications and new media at the Virginia Association of REALTORS. "That's about one-fourth of the U.S. population. Based on simple math, one-fourth of my members may already be there. Small associations don't have the money to create and cultivate an online community. We already attend the trade shows that our members attend. This is just another version of that."

"Social networking is a feature, not a destination," says Chris Anderson, author of *The Long Tail* and editor-in-chief of *Wired* magazine. "All sites going forward will have some form of social networking."

Associations have already embraced rich media as a way to communicate.

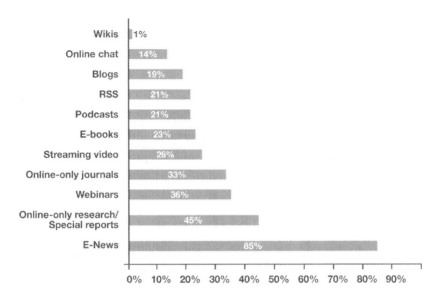

Wikis — 1%
Online chat — 14%
Blogs — 19%
RSS — 21%
Podcasts — 21%
E-books — 23%
Streaming video — 25%
Online-only journals — 33%
Webinars — 36%
Online-only research/Special reports — 45%
E-News — 85%

0% 10% 20% 30% 40% 50% 60% 70% 80% 90%

Source: 2007 E-Publishing Trends and Metrics

And they are seeing real returns on rich media activities, especially where far-flung audiences are concerned. The Million Dollar Round Table launched MDRTV with video content from its annual meeting and saw a 50 percent spike in hits from outside the United States. The next step will be to add subtitles or voice-overs.

Rich media is no guarantee of winning engagement, however, and results like those for MDRTV are based on receptiveness and relevance rather than on media channel. Rich media works when it offers different levels of participation and accommodates what people actually do online.

Rich media "takes a lot of maintenance and the topics have to be compelling," says Gary Boyler, executive director of the International Coach Federation (ICF). "It's another discipline but it's one of the services you have to offer. You see these sites with information that's a month old, a year old or older, and the same information for everyone."

Scientific associations especially still rely on their incredible libraries of research findings and data without expending much energy on helping users find it. Their sites are more repositories than interactive destinations. An exception is the American Chemical Society with its Technology Catalyst Experience, which it bills as a molecule marketplace. The network invites scientists to interact, leverage technology, and possibly find investors. It creates connections—the chance to produce new value in the world and to be recognized for that contribution. By working on both these fronts, it meets what Jeneanne Rae, president of Peer Insight, calls functional and emotional needs.

A crucial difference in the Web 2.0 world is the emotional quotient. In the past, Web sites, even very sophisticated ones, were still more about locating information or opting in to have information pushed at you. E-newsletters still are one of the most popular and cost-effective communications mediums, and most of what they do is tell you about new content on a given site. Web 2.0 wants you to have a conversation. It doesn't just ask you to communicate, it's counting on it. That means that it's not enough to just add lots of bells and whistles—cool tools attached to nothing very significant. Just like in face-to-face conversation, there needs to be genuine interest on a personal level, there needs to be a fairly clear idea about whom I'm talking to, and there needs to be an honest exchange. Theoretically, associations should be very good at this. They've been bringing people together to network forever.

LET'S TALK

More than half (52 percent) of people who go online are "inactive." They read and they go away. They may, of course, come back again and again and be very engaged with the content, but except for some mathematical record of their presence, there's no trace of their engagement (or their their lack thereof). The other half are more demonstrably engaged either because they find something interesting and relevant or because they like the medium in which it's presented. Level of engagement moves up a ladder developed by Forrester Senior Analyst Jeremiah K. Owyang, with the top rung being people who actually create content of their own (see chart next page).

The goal is not to move people up the ladder but to invite participation and engagement at each level. In a Web 2.0 world, every page is a home page and every user should find something to do. The goal is not to turn "inactives" into "joiners" or even "spectators" but to engage each user in the way they want to engage. Static content, images (both static and animate), static and interactive charts, audio content, video content, downloads of all kinds, and ample opportunity for dialog need to coexist on almost every page. A user may be inactive and still be loyal. Think of the sites you visit often, even daily, to do nothing but read the content.

"The 'mailbox members' that are more or less 90 percent of most association members, who have always been lurkers, that won't change," says Rob Wenger, chief technology officer of Washington, DC-based-Higher Logic, a provider of on-demand social networking software.

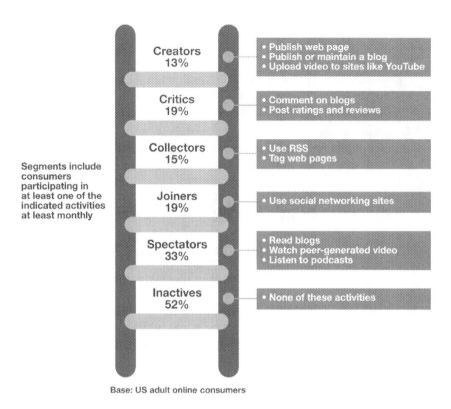

Segments include consumers participating in at least one of the indicated activities at least monthly

- Creators 13%
  - Publish web page
  - Publish or maintain a blog
  - Upload video to sites like YouTube
- Critics 19%
  - Comment on blogs
  - Post ratings and reviews
- Collectors 15%
  - Use RSS
  - Tag web pages
- Joiners 19%
  - Use social networking sites
- Spectators 33%
  - Read blogs
  - Watch peer-generated video
  - Listen to podcasts
- Inactives 52%
  - None of these activities

Base: US adult online consumers

Source: Forrester's NACTAS Q4 2006 Devices and Access Online Survey

At the same time, it is also crucial to ensure that content creators have plenty of options to evangelize for the association. These are the people who help create standards, who peer-review articles, who update wiki postings, and who are vocal in their passion for the association and its value proposition. Rich media turbocharges what these people can do.

Forrester Research analysts Charlene Li and Josh Bernoff's book, *Groundswell*, charts a phenomenon made possible by rich and social media: a group of customers who have the power to make you or break you, create or cripple your brand via their widespread social interactions. Those "creators" at the top of the engagement ladder can blog you into submission, for instance. Critics can pick your research findings apart by rating the content or expose weaknesses in your governance by posting comments. On the other hand, they can broadcast interesting ideas from your site by forwarding the text or promote your events by sending a link to the keynote speech. In short, they can create a groundswell of interest, positive or negative, without you doing anything.

Rich media and social media, like traditional journalism, can be either a great thing for your association or a very bad one. It is viral—the more your users link it to others, the more you show up on those sites and the higher your ranking on search engines. And unlike public relations and marketing, you cannot control the message or the distribution of it. Your members have always said what they think about you. Now they can say it to your face, or to thousands of other people, with the click of a mouse.

"A lot of associations have qualms about online community because there are things they just don't want to talk about," Martin says. "They've decided on a policy, for instance, but certain members want to continue the debate and the association doesn't want the debate to continue."

If, as *The Decision to Join* says, involvement is the "lifeblood" of an association but gets far less strategic attention than it deserves, rich media could be the means to involving members who are thousands of miles away and to attracting younger members. "Digital information and electronic communication technologies offer alternative ways of affiliating with others and gaining access to exploding amounts and sources of information," according to the study.

One of the simplest and potentially most powerful changes an association can make, however, has nothing to do with rich media. Improving search engine optimization on an association's site would instantly make it a more popular destination. There are many changes afoot to improve search as the Web expands beyond the current capabilities of natural and even paid search. In the meantime, however, associations rarely come up among the top results on Google and, regardless of what you'd like to think, that's where most people start a search. Long-standing, loyal members may know to come directly to your site for something, but if a Google search does not turn up your research, your data, or your meeting, a new customer will go somewhere else. A lot of association sites are not Google friendly—they are behind firewalls, they demand registration, etc. All of that impedes search. By dismantling those barriers, you let Google help you.

New technology with its arsenal of tools gives associations the opportunity "to architect a new marketplace," says Jeff De Cagna, founder of Principled Innovation, a Reston, Virginia-based association consultancy. They will, however, have to give up the illusion of control and "devolve and distribute responsibility away from the core to the edges where it needs to be." Associations can now "engage the membership in being co-creators," he says. "This is a fundamentally different way of doing it. It's always been about centralized control. If we can turn it into something that is more distributed and therefore much more distributive then I think we have a chance of moving in a new direction that would allow us to be more successful."

David Sabol, former virtual communities program developer for the Project Management Institute, says that associations "have to acknowledge that there are smart people out there and get over themselves."

PMI rolled out its social network at the end of 2008. "We'll have industry verticals, niche areas within PMBOK [Project Management Book of Knowledge], communities of interest—diversity, troubled projects, for instance, agile project management, etc.," says Mark Langley, executive vice president and chief operating officer. "It's a way of providing knowledge. That's the driving strategy of PMI."

"I'm not concerned about failure," Sabol says. "Value will be created at some level. Right now, to create a community within PMI, it's a 12-step process so they go to Facebook and create their own."

ON THE EDGE

The use of social media not only makes you look cutting edge, it forces you to *be* cutting edge.

"Social media rewards popularity, not quality or accuracy," writes blogger Jon Miller on Strictly Business (http://searchengineland.com/lands/strictly-business.php). This means that "there is an inherent push to write about trendy topics that will get links."

Your goal probably is not trendiness, but if you can't sustain a social media effort, it means one of two things: either you're unclear on the technology and have applied it badly, or you're not as cool as you thought. Your value proposition is either not compelling enough, or you're not conveying it as such, or you're not giving members the tools needed to make them part of it. The incredible diversity of associations shows the consuming interest that many people have in what seems to outsiders a very narrow subject. Rich media should make that even more interesting to more people, and if it doesn't, there's something wrong with the subject or with the way you're packaging it.

"It's worse to be bad at it than not do it at all," says Martin of the Virginia Association of REALTORS. Disagreeing that value will be created at some level, Martin feels that online community badly implemented will disappoint potential participants and drive them elsewhere.

The Society for Human Resource Management (SHRM) made the commitment to rich media with its recently launched Web site. For maximum relevance, SHRM publishes nine e-newsletters—one for compensation and benefits professionals, for instance, and another for diversity. With the launch of the new site, each issue of each e-newsletter includes an embedded video.

E-news subscribers gain relevant information in a new, dynamic medium, and SHRM gains an ever-expanding library of videos for its member site.

"You've got to build things that are appropriate to the audience," says Gary Rubin, chief publishing and e-media officer/group publisher. "Where rich media was concerned, the only thing holding us back was executing it well. It's evolved to where we can do that now."

Like it or not, the world is moving online for its communications, and those who can't keep up will not be able to win the attention—not to mention the engagement—necessary to compete. "It's beyond the capabilities of many associations," Boyler says.

The twin impediments to the reluctance to enter the online community world—clinging to the illusion of control and the inevitable hesitation of one generation to give way to the new methods of the next generation—and business practices.

"All organizations go through cycles of internal development and then development of external products and services," Langley says. "It ebbs and flows. Over the last three years, we've put business processes and management systems in place that allow us to be an always-on enterprise. We have scenario planning, dialogue at meetings and between meetings, phase gate decision making, program and portfolio management, project management. We have to do this because all of the concurrent streams of development and opportunity are almost more than we can handle. Speed is a relative concept in associations. PMI is very fast judged against other associations but judged against Google or some for-profit like that, we're very slow."

The American Society of Interior Designers spends 10 percent of its budget on technology. The American Society for Quality has nine people in its Web offerings department and thirteen in its IT department—11.5 percent of its total staff. This is far beyond a fad embraced by a few large, well-financed early adopters.

Technology either creates value or enables the creation of value, whereas traditional association communications report on value already created. Even with thirteen print publications, the American Banking Association is reporting on things that already happened—the past. Its calendar listings invite you to attend upcoming events, but the event itself is where the value will be created. Today's dynamic media make you part of the event itself, both as participant and creator. Online, you can help create the value instead of just reading about it later.

WEAK TIES BECOME STRONG

In 1973, sociologist Mark Granovetter posited the theory of the strength of weak ties. This is, thirty-five years later, the basis for online communities. Unlike traditional association membership, members of an online community may not know each other; they move in different social circles and have less overlapping knowledge. If they are active in the community, however, they can exploit those weak ties to find new opportunities, collaborators, jobs, or employees and to build a support structure, a network. There is the virtual hanging out of Facebook and the more directed pursuit of LinkedIn.

In the latter case, members have much of the same enlightened self-interest as members of a traditional association. They joined to build professional contacts that might lead to opportunity. As associations build their own online communities, members will have more overlapping knowledge than the "contacts" on LinkedIn, but they can be on opposite sides of the planet and base that knowledge on completely different sets of experience.

Even a community linked by weak ties builds up social capital, the phenomenon that promotes cooperation between community members. The permission-based process of joining encourages members to trust each other. As time passes and the community performs as expected, the members see it as a trusted source, use it more and more, and find ways to collaborate and cooperate.

There are plenty of reasons to believe that associations that successfully utilize online communities will convert weak ties to strong ties much more quickly. Online community also is a way to make the strong ties of current members even stronger:

- The social capital accrued by inviting "friends" to join an online community built atop the already-established trust of an association is extremely compelling from both a membership-value and a competitive standpoint. This is not something Facebook can match. Already one-third of Internet users belong to a professional online community, according to the 2008 Digital Future Project.

- Online community brings the "always-on" access of the Internet to associations. Members can interact 24/7 and around the world, oblivious to the office hours at headquarters or the timing of the next annual meeting.

- Social media turns your Web site into a giant data feed. The issues, comments, and discussions of an online community give the association an ear to what's really on members' minds. The organization becomes more responsive and can segment itself in relevant ways.

As long as you act on the data you gather, you've closed the loop on being member-centric. "Nurse Practitioners are only 1 percent of our membership," says Stuart Meyer, membership and marketing officer of the Emergency Nurses Association, "but they want to be active so we're going to make that possible for them and see what happens."

- Online community and Web 2.0 in general let you "create things people seek, not things that seek people," says Bud Caddell, strategist for Undercurrent, a digital think tank, and Association Growth Partners's (AGP) former director of technology and analysis. "Associations are a perfect fit for Web 2.0. They exist solely to serve their members and make the profession better. Who is going to make that happen? The 200 people that run the association or the 260,000 people that belong to it?"

- Online community is analogous to the best networking event you ever planned or attended. The conversation is so stimulating and so open, the contacts are so rich and valuable, and the potential is so great for current and future collaboration that people come again and again.

- Online community within an association creates what Meyer calls "a relationship with benefits." He says, "You already have the members, instead of someone having to recreate that, you have the content, you have events—that's the relationship with benefits."

Associations cannot be afraid that online community will cannibalize face-to-face activities. This is not a zero-sum game. The world is not divided neatly into what we do online and what we do in real life. Overextended teenagers realized immediately that online communities were a way to build and maintain relationships when there's limited opportunity for face time. Overextended professionals can do the same. Have the discussion when you have a few minutes, less time than it takes to pick up the phone or to have a meeting or to attend a three-day conference. One does not replace the other. We may connect offline with the same people with whom we connect online—or with entirely different people we would never otherwise have met. It's the quality of the relationship that matters, not the venue.

"We're moving from a 'let's build it and see who buys it' world to a 'let's pick a community and make a product they want,'" Caddell says. "Associations have the closest seat at this show, and they better make use of it."

They can also stop worrying about cannibalizing print revenues. "I don't believe in cannibalization," SHRM's Rubin says. "There's definitely a migration from print to online with advertising dollars. Would I rather that money went online somewhere else or to my online?"

MONETIZATION

The difficulty with all of B2B rich media, regardless of subject matter, is monetization. Blogs, podcasts, online video, and webcasts certainly are popular. A study by InsightExpress showed that rich media boosted unaided brand awareness by 229 percent. But except for webinars and the potential to sell research reports, the monetization of most rich media is unproven.

Part of the problem for associations is that rich media often is available only to members. It is a cost of providing services rather than a revenue generator. It can, however, be used for member acquisition and, even more lucratively, for sponsorship sales. "We already are an online community," says Jim Vick, publisher and editorial director at IEEE. "It has to work for the members but financially, we also have to engage nonmembers. Their eyeballs are just as good. If they join, it's icing on the cake. We have a member wizard on our site and we sent 12,000 people to membership last year."

Information is becoming what *Mapping the Future* calls a "profitless commodity." Web 2.0 means pennies on the dollar compared to print advertising sales at this point, but it is the only part of advertising that is growing. Revenues from and traffic to digital are enjoying double-digit growth, but print is not. That means revamping the business model and looking for both the hard and the soft ROI.

The American Composites Manufacturers have a digital version of their *Digital Matters* magazine. "The plan is to eliminate the costly postage for international magazines being sent to members and free subscribers," says Debbie Ayres, senior director, membership and communications. There is currently no additional charge for the live links within ads, but that is something ACM is considering for the future," she says. There are no plans to do away with the print version of the magazine, but "hopefully, we'll just start realizing some additional revenue for the digital version and save the costly international postage."

Most digital marketers have settled on four Web 2.0 metrics:
- Reach.
- Engagement.
- Word-of-mouth impact.
- Search visibility.

Of these, reach is the least important since quality matters more than quantity. If your goal is engagement, your success can be measured by the number of people going to the site and doing something—downloading a white paper, registering for podcasts, etc. Higher Logic is developing an algorithm to measure return on engagement. Using metrics that count actions taken rather than simple hits is critical since the user could be anyone.

The crucial question always is: what do you want users to do? Some of that drives revenues—event sign-up, credentialing inquiries, membership renewal, and so on—and some of it drives your value proposition. Digital outreach should be compelling because of its tight connection to your mission and all the ways in which you deliver it. Using rich media to elicit action is a tactic that gives you the metrics to show you're accomplishing your goals. The value of all media is organization-specific. It could be market research for one organization, competitive analysis for another, or communication for a third. The trick is to find the one that meets your goals and suits your brand.

There is not yet a working revenue model for social media. "It is entirely conceivable that social networking, like web-mail, will never make oodles of money," says March 22, 2008 issue of *The Economist*. "That, however, in no way detracts from its enormous utility.... If there is no pressure to make a business out of it, it can remain intimate and discreet."

DIALOG, NOT MONOLOG

One of the principal advantages of Web 2.0 is that, when it works well, the users themselves refresh the site with new content and active dialogue, reducing both time and expense for the owner of the URL. Conference attendees can upload photos, discuss the speeches, rate trade show offerings, and much, much more. Comments to blogs, articles, white papers, etc., add context and liveliness to otherwise static content. There is more than a little trepidation about the attendant loss of control but, as De Cagna notes on his blog (www.principledinnovation.com/blog), "we never had it in the first place."

Standards-setting associations rely on the expertise of members to create and constantly raise the bar on accepted standards. User-generated content has always been central to what they do. As Jim Vick, publisher and editorial director of IEEE Media, says, "If we don't have the member pushing stuff into the front end of the pipe, we've got nothing. Member-generated content doesn't scare us. Anyone can publish. The value a professional publisher adds is by vetting that content and putting their equivalent of the Good Housekeeping Seal on it."

Given IEEE's struggle to retain young members, however, that constant inflow of new ideas may be drying up—unless the association can unlock the secret to online community in which younger members are more likely to participate.

According to Forrester Research, 60 percent of young people use social networking on a weekly basis and 40 percent check those sites daily. Associations looking to attract younger members instantly appeal to a new generation by using the communications tools young people already use to manage much of their lives. And that is a crucial difference between social media and basic digital media. Digital media is an online version of print—a huge leap in itself. Rich media and social media are how some people manage their lives. Bill payments, baby pictures, meeting schedules, conference calls, webinars, book recommendations—you name it, it's online, increasingly mobile and, with Twitter, can even appear in blocks of fewer than 140 characters. It's a multitasking world, borderless, without time zones, but manageable with the right software and a broadband connection.

"Social media is like manna from heaven," De Cagna writes in *101 Things About Associations We Must Change* (www.alwaysdoneitthatway.com). "By introducing greater richness and texture to the discourse we have with our most crucial stakeholders, we can quite possibly renovate for the better the eroding value propositions of traditional association membership offers and volunteer leadership participation. But this will happen only if we can get out of our own way."

In fact, vetting the content, as Vick says, may be part of associations' problem. It only perpetuates the illusion of control.

Publishing content is "all about push," Anderson says. "We talk, you listen. We publish, you read. That's great for the mass but terrible for everything else. We have to switch from publishing to community management. This is a new market of the neglected. The content that has not been vetted—is it good, is it relevant, is it the best of its type? The Web doesn't care; the audience decides."

Member-to-member sharing—the essence of an association—via something as basic as a Listserv or as sophisticated as an online community catapults an association into a new era of networking. It is the association functioning in real time with little resource commitment from association staff itself. Associations had user-generated content long before everyone else started talking about it.

There are liability concerns in allowing members to become authors in an open forum, of course, but they are vastly overestimated by associations, according to De Cagna. "Certainly some of that exists and you can't get around it," he says, but that should not be an excuse not to embrace the possibilities.

Someone hacked the EduCAUSE social network in early 2008 and posted an inappropriate video. "We use a spam filter," says Rebecca Granger, CAE, director of information technology at EduCAUSE, "but that won't catch the binary stuff." A huge internal debate ensued about whether to use an equivalent of the strike-through on a blog—leave the offending content, but show that you deem it offensive. That was not an option given the nature of the video. They talked about censoring and moderating. "We talked about whether we were trying to protect our members from each other or protect ourselves from them," Granger says. "What we were trying to do was protect them from offensive content." EduCAUSE took the video down and developed a trust algorithm: if you're a newcomer (joeblow@gmail.com, for instance) you do not have the same rights as a frequent poster. You move up the trust barometer until you earn the right to post images, videos, and other content from there.

Rich media invites user-generated content but does not guarantee that it will appear. Using a community manager to seed content on other sites, to maximize search engine optimization, and to constantly scan metrics for adjustments based on results is the only way to make good on the investment new media demands.

Association Growth Partners (AGP) employs a full-time community manager for its client, PMI. That job entails scanning the horizon all day, every day, for homes for PMI content. A group of PMI members created a blog to critique each month's cover of *PM Network*, for instance. By linking to that—seeding content on that and other sites—the magazine's contents show up on a lot more screens, PMI's search results improve, and its reach expands.

"You have to have someone dedicated to updating the Web," says Boyler of ICE.

Rich media as it is currently used by associations is, at best, an interim step. It is, however, crucial to reaching the next step: the reinvention of the association. "Social media are the antithesis of bureaucracy. Social media are pure creation," De Cagna says. "People are now able to organize online without the need for associations. Membership has been redefined by what is happening online."

"This is their chance to reinvent themselves," says RIMS's Andy Steggles, who also is the creator of the Association of Associations on Facebook.

In one of the essays in his book, *Managing in the Next Society*, Peter Drucker posits the concept of "routinization." Collectively, we tend to use new technologies to automate what was done in the past without questioning whether or not the technology affords us new opportunities for change. People have always communicated, and now we have e-mail, for instance.

Simply using new technological tools to do the same things associations have always done is not reinvention. If younger members aren't interested in joining, dressing things up in a new coat will not convince them. If you're willing to sell individual products rather than membership to global audiences, those audiences will take the technology that makes those products available and customize it to their own needs. Associations have much to learn from members about what they want and what media they want it in.

Perhaps the reason that so many associations are sitting on the fence about social media is the realization that it will change everything. Top-to-bottom transformation powered by technology is the future of associations.

"This is the greatest opportunity any of us has ever had," Steggles says. "Most associations are so afraid but it's not doom and gloom. This is an incredible opportunity. Our membership is very risk averse, obviously. But the bigger risk is doing nothing."

Virtual Meetings

FactPoint Group conducted a study of two hundred virtual events organized by Unisfair, totaling nearly three thousand sponsors and five hundred thousand attendees. It found that the average virtual event has a registration of 3,102 people and an attendance of 1,587. Sponsors received almost 350 leads, and attendees spent an average of two and a half hours at the event, visiting sixteen locations and completing at least five downloads.

Don Best, director of marketing at Unisfair, admits that virtual events never will replace live ones and that virtual events can't offer the exotic location that is one of the three main reasons for event attendance. However, technology has progressed to support the other two: to gain knowledge and to network. Event planners are using virtual events to augment physical events, Best says.

The Risk and Insurance Management Society has an annual conference, which consumes 65 percent of its budget. This year, it will host a virtual conference à la Second Life. "It's a $30,000 experiment," says Andy Steggles, RIMS's chief information officer. "It will last three days. We'll have pre-conference social events. They can take a boat ride, for instance. Giveaways. You have to insert a plug-in and because many of our members have very strict security at work, they may not be able to participate or will have to participate from their home computer. We just want to see what will happen."

The so-called Webvolution is the evolution of the Internet "into a three-dimensional virtual world in which people, as avatars, interact, work and collaborate," according to Karl Kapp, assistant director of the Institute for Interactive Technologies and a professor professor of instructional technology at Bloomsburg University, and Tony O'Driscoll, professor at North Carolina State University's Jenkins

Graduate School of Management. Further, it is "beginning to permeate the learning and development field," according to *Learning Circuits*, the e-learning portal of the American Society of Training and Development.

Most training still is done in classrooms, which limits the field's ability to take advantage of technology. Professors Kapp and O'Driscoll say we are missing the opportunity to forever change the teaching, training, and learning processes.

"Virtual reality environments are already proving useful for collaborative learning events such as role playing," write Kapp and O'Driscoll on *Learning Circuits*.

Online education already is creating new revenue streams for associations. IEEE generates fifteen to twenty thousand dollars per technology webinar. The editor is compensated with a commission on participation.

Another creative use of virtual meetings is the career fair held by the Regulatory Affairs Professionals Society. As an experiment, RAPS hosted "several hundred" job seekers, according to Zachary Brousseau, manager of communications. Thirteen companies took part. Attendees could go to each online "booth" and start a conversation with the company representative. Well over a month later, attendees could come back to schedule meetings with prospective employers. Based on the success, another, larger virtual career fair will take place in the future.

Open Access

Open access, says Jim Vick of IEEE Media, is "scaring the hell out of us right now." The debate began in 2001 when George Soros' Open Society Institute called for all scholarly work to be available free of charge online. Since 34 percent of associations publish scholarly journals, incur the expense of peer-review and publishing, and reap healthy revenues in the process, this got their attention. According to the University of Illinois at Urbana-Champaign library, journal expenditures among North American research libraries jumped by 273 percent between 1986 and 2004. The cost of a journal increased by 188 percent, outstripping inflation four-fold. Last fall, after changing publishers, the American Anthropological Association upped the price of its two flagship journals by 86 percent (*American Anthropologist*) and 145 percent (*American Ethnologist*).

The Federal Research Public Access Act, conceived in 2007, would require that federally funded research become publicly available online within six months of publication. The Act limits this to eleven government agencies with external research budgets of more than $100 million annually. The EU followed in January of 2008 with a similar mandate.

"If you've taken government money, it's a different story," Vick says, "but the rest of us have to make money somehow."

The debate comes down sharply on each side of that issue. Those opposed say that open access will hit all research publishers, especially nonprofits, very hard. Those in favor say that providing free access after a short embargo period to protect subscription revenue is an equally viable option and that anything that speeds up scientific communication speeds up scientific progress.

"The data clearly show that free access and profitability are not mutually exclusive," according to the American Society for Cell Biology's position paper. All research articles published in ASCB's flagship journal, *Molecular Biology of the Cell*, is provided to anyone visiting its Web site two months after publication. Based on seven years of experience, ASCB says that the embargo is enough to ensure the publication's revenues and support the costs of research without slowing scientific progress.

As the debate continues and more and more journals go open access, publishers are experimenting with hybrids, looking for better and simpler pricing models and looking to cut costs. A lobbying initiative, called PRISM, made by the American Chemical Society, the Association of American Publishers (AAP/PSP), and the International Association of Scientific, Technical and Medical Publishers fell very flat, very loudly. The directors of MIT and Columbia University presses both resigned from AAP/PSP's executive council, and nine scientific publishers disavowed the initiative.

The objection is not to the idea of open access but to the destruction of an entrenched business model. A study on the operational costs of peer-reviewed journals found that it is easier for nonprofits to find a financial model that supports open access than for a commercial publisher, but the larger the nonprofit, the more difficult it becomes. Sustainable revenues are still available, but they come from authors, subsidies, and advertisers rather than subscriptions.

Facilitation Case Study

The American Society of Mechanical Engineers (ASME) launched its communities of practice (CoP) in 2004. "Facilitators and beta users were handpicked from among our younger members and key volunteers," says Diedra Hackley, manager, unit support. Today, whoever suggests a new community provides the name of a facilitator—usually themselves.

ASME provides a facilitator's guide and a private community that separates the functionality of the facilitator from that of the regular user. That private community enables facilitators to help each other solve problems with a minimum of ASME staff resources.

Demonstrations were held at the annual meeting, but Hackley says that monthly webinars by an experienced facilitator would have been helpful. Regular meetings online and educational sessions with a speaker as well as meetings with other members who use online communities keep facilitators motivated. Making sure members know of the CoPs and fuel them with a constant stream of new content is the biggest problem.

Recognition is part of the payoff for volunteer facilitators. Highlight them on the CoP home page, create awards for most active, most improved and the like, and feature them in monthly e-newsletters.

By the Numbers

- China has overtaken the United States with the most online users in the world. At the end of 2008, China had 280 million Internet users.

- *Baidu*, the Chinese language search engine, ranks third worldwide, behind Google and Yahoo!.

- There are more than one hundred million blogs, an estimated thirteen million of which are actively updated.

- Traffic to social networking sites has grown 34 percent since 2007 to 530 million, representing two out of every three Internet users.

- Video is the number-one online entertainment format.

Among adults, according to Forrester Research:

- 22 percent read blogs.

- 40 percent check user reviews before making an online purchase.

- In 2001, more than 50 percent of all business meetings were face-to-face; by 2004, only slightly more than 40 percent were face-to-face.

Questions

- What percentage of dues-based members is inactive?

- What percentage of free online community members is inactive?

- What is the average membership tenure for each?

- Are online communities like associations, or are they simply knowledge-sharing resources?

Chapter 4

Value Proposition

Show me the money.

—Cuba Gooding Jr.'s character in *Jerry Maguire*

When you hear *value proposition*, what comes to mind? For those who staff associations, the term often is used interchangeably with *mission*. For them, the mission of the association is its value proposition. Members—current and potential—however, may think of something else, something more overtly sales oriented.

One of Association Growth Partner's value propositions is to produce the best association publications in the world. Our mission is to be the best custom publisher and relationship marketing agency in the world. The two are related, but the former is one of the things we take to market. It's a line in the sand against our competitors. When we're asked to give the "elevator pitch," we don't spout the mission. We're selling outsourced content services, and the value proposition asks for the sale.

Mission is who you are. Value proposition is what you get paid for.

There are three components to a value proposition, according to Geoffrey Moore's *Crossing the Chasm*:

1.   The product itself, i.e., membership in your association

2. The target customer, i.e., current and potential members

3. Target applications, i.e., the products and services that deliver the promised value

Those three comprise "something one can sell," Moore writes. He adds three qualitative must-haves to that:

1. A strategic capability that was previously unavailable and thereby provides a dramatic competitive advantage in a prime operational area

2. A radical productivity improvement in an area that is already well understood

3. A visible, verifiable, significant reduction in total overall operating costs

The first thing that strikes me about those must-haves is how urgent they are. They are put-up or shut-up mandates, very much the things that would make potential members think, "I *must* do this." Without those compelling, quantifiable deliverables, membership in your association might be nice, but it won't be valuable.

"When headhunters call me, they always say that they're looking for someone who can grow membership for an association with flat or no growth," says Mark Langley, executive vice president and chief operating officer of the Project Management Institute (PMI). "I always tell them that that's not a strategy. What do you have of value? If all you've got is some random information and networking, that's not so valuable."

The proposition that associations take to new markets, the "something one can sell," is becoming smaller. The unbundling already discussed leaves associations selling the target applications, pieces of the whole. This works as a market entry tactic but cannot sustain the association unless it can sell a lot of smaller things to many, many people.

"There are a lot of people who are interested, but not to the level of membership," says Chris Anderson, author of *The Long Tail* and editor-in-chief of *Wired* magazine. "We've always focused on what most people want rather than what lots of people want. The future is the aggregation of the 'many small' rather than the one or two big."

"It's not just a question of what people are willing to pay," says Jeff De Cagna, founder of Principled Innovation, "but of what they're willing to pay for."

Unbundling also is a way to attract younger members.

"New members are less interested in the gold standard that we've established," Langley says. "They want what they want and if they come to our site and don't find it, they'll go right by us. The legacy members find the gold standard more important."

Rewriting the value proposition is the only way to find a sustainable financial model for associations. They must define "something one can sell" as larger than individual applications but potentially totally different from membership as it is currently known.

WHAT'S IT WORTH TO YOU?

For an association, there are two sides to the value proposition: the members' value to you and your value to them. The first is quantitative; the second, more qualitative. Their value to you is revenues and involvement—without participation from the members, you don't exist, and they need to pay to be involved. Your value to them is the unique experience you provide.

Calculating the quantitative side of that equation is less straightforward than it sounds. The simplest calculation for customer lifetime value (CLTV), according to the American Society of Association Executives, is to look at only the lifetime value from dues:

$$1 / (1\text{-}R) \times \text{Dues revenue} = \text{CLTV}$$

R equals the retention rate. If retention is 80 percent, for instance, 1 minus 0.8 equals 0.2; 1 divided by 0.2 equals 5. If your dues are $160, CLTV is $800.

Today, when only slightly more than one-third of revenues come from dues, non-dues revenue can't be ignored in calculating CLTV. That calculation is:

Average member tenure in years

× average dues
+ Non-dues revenue
+ Conference attendance
+ Publication purchases
= CLTV

Things become more complicated depending on whether the association is an individual membership organization or a trade.

There also are trends that impact how CLTV is measured.

• Experts are including more life-stage factors. For associations, this means the member's *career stage*. Student members at the International Interior Design Association (IIDA), for instance, are crucial to building future members in an organization where the average member is only thirty-seven years old. The business model does not, however, support providing them with unlimited access to products and services at their reduced membership rate. The CLTV of tenure would seem to trump everything—number of years multiplied by dues is higher the longer someone belongs. But at what point in an interior design career does the member participate most heavily, buy more publications, sign up for more courses, attend more conferences? In actual fact, career stage may be a greater determiner of CLTV than tenure.

- There is a greater emphasis on *retention* as a factor in calculating CLTV. The cost of retention is part of a membership marketing budget, but it is cheaper and easier to keep a member than to acquire a new one. So the lifetime value of a retained member should be higher, and the multiplier should go up the longer that person stays a member.

- Members who *refer* new members also have a higher lifetime value. Their CLTV cannot be calculated based simply on products sold. Arlene Farber Sirkin of the Washington Resource Consulting Group cites the example of an association member who recruited more than two hundred new members in the course of his own tenure. Because recruiters like these save the association acquisition money, their value is higher than someone who never refers a friend and helps convert them to membership.

A better, more qualitative calculation is:

CLTV based on non-dues revenue calculation above
$\times$ Volunteer hours at $X per hour
$+$ Career-stage multiplier
$+$ Retention multiplier
$+$ Dues from member referrals
$=$ True membership value

There also is the metric called *evangelism*. Remember the "creators" from the top of the engagement ladder in Chapter 3? They exhibit what *Creating Customer Evangelists*, by Ben McConnell and Jackie Huba calls "the highest form of customer loyalty."

According to the book (adapted here for associations), there are six tenets that organizations that successfully create evangelism adhere to:

- Customer-plus delta

  Continuously gather member feedback

- Napsterized knowledge

  Share knowledge freely

- Build the buzz

  Expertly build word-of-mouth networks

- Create community

  Encourage communities of members to meet and share

- Bite-size it

  Devise specialized, smaller offerings to get members to bite

- Create a cause

  Sell dreams instead of products

There are questions related to each tenet that can lead to metrics to calculate customer lifetime value.

Customer-plus delta Continuously gather member feedback	• How many ideas for new products and services were gathered from member feedback? • How much revenue did those new products and services generate? • How many problems were identified and solved? • How did member suggestions improve quality? • Did the suggestions save money? If so, how much?
Napsterized knowledge Share knowledge freely	• Do members mention your association online? How often? • Do they forward publications and/or articles? • What is the referral or pass-along rate of your e-newsletter(s)? • Do any of your members have their own blog? If so, do they mention the association?

Build the buzz Expertly build word-of-mouth networks	• How do new members say they discovered you? • Which organizations visit your Web site most often? • Are they "qualified," i.e., the sort of organizations from which your members come? • Are they organizations that your members also belong to or work for? • What part of the world are they in? • Do credentialed members fuel word-of-mouth networks more than non-credentialed members? • Are members advocating at a grassroots level in line with your advocacy agenda?
Create community Encourage communities of members to meet and share	• How many members' e-mail addresses do you have? • Are subscriptions increasing, decreasing or flat? • How active are chapters, special interest groups, etc.? • Do those members solicit new members? • If you have an e-mail discussion group (Listserv), how many members are there? • Do frequent posters pull in other members? • If you have an online community, how many members are there? • How active is it? • Are there online communities that attract your members? Do you link to them and they to you? • Do members bring guests to conferences?

Bite-size it Devise specialized, smaller offerings to get members to bite	• How many prospective members have sampled your member benefits? • How many did you convert? • What's the referral rate? • Do your specialized offerings appeal to a specific career stage to maximize cross-sell?
Create a cause Sell dreams instead of products	• How many prospective members contact you based on your mission? • How many did you convert? • How many members belong to your association exclusively? • How many members apply for staff positions?

A customer's lifetime value goes up and up based on these factors. Cheryl Durst, executive director of the International Interior Design Association (IIDA), keeps track of how many members contact the association to ask questions, which members, and what kind of questions. This is one way of achieving all six tenets. "It gives me ideas about products and services. It lets me know how involved an individual is. It tells me who they're talking to."

"Customer evangelism is a gift," write McConnell and Huba. "Your evangelists must be treated like the royalty they are." In one association, members compete to win places on the retention committee because, for every member retained, they win points toward attendance at the annual cruise.

VALUE, NOT PRICE

Value is not always a number. The value of *The Economist*, for instance, has little to do with the hard costs of paper, printing, mailing, salaries, etc., and more to do with the quality of the reporting and writing, the user-friendly design, and its reputation as one the most read business publications in the world. Circulation increased by 70,000 in 2006 and 81,000 in 2007 while readership at competing magazines was flat. *The Economist* provides "an elite analysis of the week's news and larger trends," according to *The State of the News Media 2008*, a value proposition not easily duplicated.

Members may complain about dues—and certainly about increases—but low cost comes with a perception of low value. The subscription price for *The Economist* is three times that of competing news magazines, and it is one of only two publications in its category that is growing.

Calculating the members' value to you and your value to them in hard dollars neglects the intangibles. A trade association must attract the senior executives from its member companies, rather than have them delegate participation. Those decision makers have more value to the association than middle managers. A professional association must attract members with the technical or scientific skills to sit on standards committees and help develop credentials. Otherwise, the proposition on which membership rests won't deliver.

How valuable such members are goes beyond how many publications they buy, how often they renew, or even how many new members they refer.

HOW MUCH ARE YOU WORTH?

Calculating your value to members is not limited to the benefits list on your Web site. If, as *Where the Winners Meet* says, association membership increases an individual's chances for professional success, that has a value that is incalculable.

But other things about the association value proposition are being undermined by the triple threat of globalization, technology, and demographics. Competition from heretofore unfamiliar sources is taking associations outside their traditional ecosystem. Associations that count on loyalty for revenues—from ad sales to conference attendance—will have to step it up just to survive. Remaining a viable competitive force will need to go substantially beyond that.

"While associations remain important and effective assimilators, repositories and sources of information within a specific trade or profession, this is no longer a strong enough value proposition, on its own, to convince modern stakeholders to join or stay as a member," says Terrance A. Barkan, founder of Association Global Services. Faster, more nimble for-profit competitors have stepped into that space and stolen the franchise on conferences—for instance, educational seminars and the like. They vie not only for participants but for speakers, trade show exhibitors, and sponsors. Information is becoming a profitless commodity. The "ownership" of a given industry or profession is no longer the automatic purview of an association but rather a competitive advantage waiting to be lost.

"If you look at SIA [Security Industry Association]," says Andy Steggles, chief information officer of the Risk and Insurance Management Society

(RIMS), "Reed Elsevier gives SIA a free booth at its ISC trade show. Meanwhile, the association has lost the opportunity to create its own event. The event only drives value one week a year so Reed Elsevier launched ISC365community.com. Now they've stolen that opportunity from the association."

In the old days, a company would buy a membership for every employee at a given level. More and more, dues, conference attendance, publication purchase, and seminar enrollment come out of the individual member's pocket. "Companies who now buy multiple memberships may cut back to only one," says IIDA's Durst. "Companies that pay for membership in more than one association may choose one or the other. If we have to prove our value to each and every individual, things become a lot tougher all around."

Jeremy Gutsche, founder of TrendHunter.com, says that there is only one really important message associations have to learn. "Relentlessly obsess about your story. Relentlessly. Obsess. Everyone, everyone, everyone must be able to articulate the value proposition. And they should be able to say it in seven words or less. The benefits of that are differentiation and empowerment."

The way to remain valuable is to make yourself indispensable. Provide what people actually need every day. Some examples:

- One of the Metals Service Center Institute's major research efforts, the Executive Chartbook, is an industry and financial benchmarking tool. Member companies submit their balance sheets and income statements, tonnage shipped, number of employees, etc., online. That generates 150 financial ratios compared to other companies. "You can do a very deep detailed job of seeing how you stack up," says Chris Marti, director of research. "How do I get better? What would better look like? You would never have access to this kind of work unless you're a large public company. Most of our members are private."

- "As more corporations hire [executive] coaches," says Gary Boyler, executive director of the International Coach Federation, "credentials are preferred if not required."

- "Design is segregated within university curricula," Durst says. Design graduates "never had access to business courses, to the social sciences. We provide them with that broader context that they have to have to succeed in business."

- "We're more market-focused than member-focused," says Langley of PMI. "We develop products and services specific to a market rather than an existing member. We discovered this opportunity as we went global. Most associations approach it with what they're selling. Our board focuses on the member and the market rather than the one or the other. We can build a model to fit the market."

Credentialing and standards are *the* indispensable association services. They are competitive advantages that associations retain, and not ones that can easily be duplicated by for-profit competitors. As independent third parties with no profit motive, associations will always be the place companies look to set global standards for products and expertise.

"We developed the CAPM for those who have a role on a project team but will never be the team leader, never be the project manager," Langley says. "You'll always have a higher success rate when there's a PMP [Project Management Professional] leading the team but this drives it down within the team itself."

The business model for standards and credentials at the Association Connecting Electronics Industries (IPC) is fairly typical. A small technical staff works with volunteers on various committees. The sale of hard copies—twenty to one hundred dollars, with members getting a 50 percent discount—pays for the overhead, meetings, and other expenses. Although the revenues are important, "our members have identified our standards as the most important benefit of membership," says Kim Sterling, CAE and marketing vice president of IPC.

Trade associations provide a different sort of value than credentials. "Trade associations, especially in capital-intensive industries with low multiples on Wall Street, can find a major source of member value by helping their members improve the cost of capital," according to *The Future of the Competitive Association*. For example, a trade association member company improves its productivity or optimal capital structure based on the experiences of its peers, thereby reducing its cost of capital and improving its multiple relative to the industry average.

"There are two key differences between associations that give members superior value and those that don't," according to the report:

1. A compelling value proposition

2. Creating product and service offerings that solve those needs better than anywhere else—faster, less expensively, more effectively, etc.

"Keeping the value proposition superior requires that associations find ways to market, sell, produce and deliver services in ways that can't easily be imitated," the report says.

Maybe there should be a new way of looking at the whole thing: return on value (ROV).

THE ROV OF NETWORKING

Communicate the value of networking by capturing and codifying what happens in the hallways at your conferences. This is not eavesdropping, but making sure that the association is the broker through which things happen and that members know and trust that. Take what is offline and, in a completely confidential way, put it online.

Find and reward the efforts of your best networkers, the ones who close the most deals with other members, gain promotions, hire off your job board, or tap fellow members for advice and counsel.

- The Healthcare Financial Management Association runs thirty to thirty-three pages of classified ads in its monthly magazine, *hfm*, 95 percent of them job listings. The association can charge a premium for them because of the very focused niche of thirty-four thousand member/readers. "There is so much churn in healthcare," says Paul Bielat, national sales director, "but this is a very qualified pool of searchers and of jobs, upper echelon jobs." There are eighty thousand subscribers to its *Career Opportunities* e-newsletter, ten thousand to its *Business of Caring* e-newsletter for nurses, and fifty-five thousand monthly page views of its online job bank.

- As the metals industry became a darling of Wall Street, the Metals Service Center Institute (MSCI) became the place where companies interested in being acquired and investors interested in acquiring met. This highly sensitive information could only be trusted to a disinterested third party.

THE ROV OF ADVOCACY

If the association is a successful advocate legislatively, at a grassroots level and in the C-suite, everyone in the profession or industry benefits. You've raised all boats, not just those of your members. Public relations and search engine optimization through blogs and other rich media bring nonmember attention to the value of being part of shaping that agenda. Using Twitter for PR blasts on legislation keeps members apprised of what's going on, adds urgency, and positions your association at the nexus of activity.

- Dirk Van Dongen, president of the National Association of Wholesaler-Distributors, organized a grassroots effort in the 2004 election. The association developed the Washington Action Network, a database that lists any personal relationships members have with members of Congress. They listed 433 personal contacts in 435 Congressional districts. They put teams in place for races they cared about, resulting in the election of Richard Burr to defeat former Clinton Chief of Staff Erskine Bowles in South Carolina and John Thune to defeat Senate Minority Leader Tom Daschle, a huge coup for a federation of more than one hundred mostly small line-of-trade associations. The teams raised nearly half a million dollars for each candidate.

- Dan DiMicco, vice chairman and CEO of Nucor Corp. and a past board member of MSCI, organized grassroots events at NASCAR tracks around the Southeast to advocate for American manufacturing jobs and the less-than-level playing field on trade. Nine such events attracted between twenty-five and thirty thousand people.

THE ROV OF KNOWLEDGE

"As knowledge becomes more specialized," says Jeff De Cagna, founder of Principled Innovation, "people will need to be able to find things, to go more deeply into the niches that are necessary to their work."

- The Project Management Book of Knowledge was released in 1995 and has sold 1.5 million copies in eleven languages. But what is the value of that knowledge? As Steve Fahrenkrog, director of knowledge delivery at PMI, says, "Whenever anyone anywhere in the world thinks of project management, they should think of us." Becoming the vocabulary used on the hundreds of construction sites in Dubai, showcasing those sites on DVD, running them as a loop on your Web site, and broadcasting them live at your annual conference makes their value obvious.

- The Society for Human Resource Management runs webcasts year-round, free to members. These Webcasts generate thirteen to nineteen thousand dollars in sponsorship money but, more importantly, attract up to seven thousand members. "You've got to build what members are interested in," says Gary Rubin, SHRM's chief publishing and e-media officer. There is no danger of cannibalizing other offerings, he says. "The cannibalization comes when vendors want to reach your constituency through a Webcast and you don't offer it, so they buy it from your competitors."

THE ROV OF BEING SPECIAL

There is enormous value to transparency, but there is an equal or greater value to exclusivity.

- The Conference Board has two thousand corporate members worldwide and has always functioned as a largely off-the-record body. Research Councils in vertical disciplines set their own agenda, meet in private, and are kept to a strict limit as to size. The Conference Board organizes all of that and, for its part, garners its research agenda from what those executives say behind closed doors. The association keeps its finger firmly on the pulse of business trends and can be first to market with an analysis of them. Members themselves enjoy the private reality of being trendsetters and market movers.

- Bob Weidner, executive director of MSCI, is a voracious reader and has created his own book group, sending copies of new, interesting titles to a select group of members.

THE ROV OF MEANING

One of the principles of successful branding is to stand for something. The chance to be part of making the world a better, safer place is a compelling value proposition. In a global context where volunteering is little known, selling the value of a higher purpose needs to be made more compelling. China already shows a preference for organizations with strong social responsibility initiatives. "Look past selling them stuff and toward delivering value to the country," says Rohit Talwar, CEO of the think tank Fast Future. "Only organizations doing positive things for the environment and CSR [corporate social responsibility] in China go to the front of the queue. They are not 'stealing' knowledge. They are looking to develop their own country. If you're in this for the long term, you will be part of the build and, therefore, part of the payoff."

- The American Society of Civil Engineers lobbies extensively. "Too many people get hung up on governance issues, like not enough members vote in the elections," says Pat Natale, CAE and ASCE executive director. "Most members trust the 'groupies,' the ones that are involved. They don't care about that stuff. They care about the products and services, the lobbying, the publications. The average member doesn't care about the board, how often they meet. They care about what's in it for them. What we've done for the profession, for young engineers coming out of school."

THE ROV OF SIMPLICITY

"Cacophony" is the word that always comes to mind when I think of modern life. Content bombardment leaves us struggling for time and a little peace and quiet. Our lives may not be substantially more complex than our parents' lives were, but they move demonstrably faster and are accompanied by a lot of noise, both relevant and extraneous.

"It's not enough to argue for relevance," De Cagna says. "If we're still discussing whether or not we're relevant, we're in trouble. That is a losing argument in the marketplace. Everyone is in the position these days of needing to disregard a considerable amount of relevant information because they simply don't have the time, energy or attention to deal with it all. Part of the opportunity for associations is to help people find what they're looking for and deal with what they're going through."

Putting hard numbers next to these ROV categories can be done. Efficient, trackable, verifiable metrics on marketing communications are absolutely possible. Acting on those metrics to adjust not just the communications but the value proposition behind them is often the missing step.

The *7 Measures of Success* study says that great associations have a thorough understanding of their mission and that mission is very concrete. The mission is segmented into areas of need with products and services developed specifically for each segment. The accent is not on how profitable those products and services are—revenues are the means rather than the end—but on how well they help achieve the mission.

"Areas of need" would be redefined as the value propositions that take the association to market. Members must be able to see how those propositions will provide both strategic capability that they don't have and striking competitive advantage that they need. They need to see how a proposition will take something that they already do and drastically improve productivity, and it must be clear that all of this will fall to the bottom line in hard numbers. That is tangible value that will flow both ways, from association to members, and members to association.

Value Proposition in Europe

Membership Recruitment and Retention in Europe 2005, a study by The Association Gateway covering European associations, found that most Europeans (54 percent) join associations for business networking. Access to best practices (49 percent), industry news (49 percent), and education (43 percent) follow closely.

For trade associations, those in manufacturing industries value the combined buying power. But relatively few members see social networking, job boards, or special offers as reasons to join.

For professional associations, members and potential members say that associations need to give a better cost-benefit analysis to justify dues.

What the study calls "member care" should include regular personal contact, relevant and timely information, and encouragement to be actively involved.

Study respondents preferred electronic communications to printed (79 percent to 38 percent), and poor communication was one of the most common reasons for not renewing membership. A major threat to renewal is better service elsewhere. But by far the biggest reason for resigning from an association is a poor return on investment.

This is contradicted by findings in *The Decision to Join* that cover American associations. About half of study respondents did not renew memberships because of changes in their careers or their lives rather than a failure on the association's part. In all cases—geography, gender, age—involvement was the key to retention. "If former members are thought of as being dead," says the study, "the uninvolved are close to comatose. And from that delightful imagery, involvement might be thought of as the lifeblood of an association, which therefore deserves much more strategic attention than it gets."

Free Membership

Fred Simmons of Gulo Solutions writes on the Gulo blog (www.gulosolutions.com) that soon associations will offer free membership. Revenues will come from volume, similar to an advertising sales model—the more eyeballs, the more valuable to advertisers, sponsors, etc.

By the Numbers

Dues as a percentage of total association revenues:

1953	95.7%
1977	52.3%
1999	40.9%
2007	37.7%
Trade	41.4%
IMO	35.1%
International/national	34.3%
Regional/state/local	45.6%

Source: The American Society of Association Executives *Operating Ratio Report*, 13th edition

Chapter 5

Branding

i'm lovin' it™

—McDonald's Corporation

Golden arches—the world is covered with golden arches. You might be able to order McMolletes or a McArabia. The person behind the counter may be wearing a head scarf. Ronald might be Asian. Paying your bill will fuel The Big Mac Index, a leading indicator of socioeconomic progress from *The Economist*. But you know what to expect from McDonald's: it will be affordable, clean, safe, and quick. It will be red and gold. It will be kid- and senior-friendly. Regardless of the language, it will be American, though locally staffed and probably locally owned and operated (as are 70 percent of McDonald's restaurants worldwide). McDonald's serves more than fifty-two million people at thirty thousand local restaurants in more than one hundred countries every day. The brand comes through in every one of those transactions. The golden arches themselves are not the brand, but when you see them, all that other stuff—affordable, red, American—comes through loud and clear.

When Imagination Publishing—the parent company of Association Growth Partners—published *McDonald's@50,* an anniversary coffee-table book, we went to brand school with the best. We learned:

- No successful brand can be narrowly defined. If McDonald's was just hamburgers, it wouldn't be a household name.

- The logo matters, but it does not constitute the brand.

- Even the most American brand can be accepted and embraced internationally and, indeed, become local.

- Branding is a constant, relentless pursuit.

"Branding has just come to associations," says Gary Boyler, executive director of the International Coach Federation (ICF). "The first step is to realize you have a brand, then you have to define it and get everyone on board as to the value and the benefits."

A brand is the complete relationship formed by an organization and its customers. "A brand is a promise of, in this case, consistent quality," Boyler says. "It's got to be something that you can deliver consistently wherever you are."

If your mission is your reason for being, your brand is the emotional attachment people form with that mission. It is how they feel about you. "People fall in love with brands," Alina Wheeler writes in *Designing Brand Identity.* "They trust them, develop strong loyalties, buy them and believe in their superiority."

Many associations do not realize—or only now are waking up to—the strength of their brand.

Power may come from *reputation.* The government of India wants all of its thousands of inspectors trained and certified by the Bethesda, Maryland-based Academy of Certified Hazardous Materials Managers (ACHMM). With a staff of two, ACHMM cannot possibly fulfill this request without the in-country implementation of a local partner, but this example demonstrates the power of the association's brand all over the world.

Power certainly comes from *dependability,* the certainty that the promise will be fulfilled. The Conference Board holds 120 conferences a year around the world. There is a similar nature to them—always a break at mid-morning, sessions of a certain length, always in a certain caliber hotel—but the quality of the speakers and of the audience is the brand promise. You know what you will get when you go to a Conference Board meeting, small or large. Never disappointing you is their brand, not the blue torch logo that appears on everything they do.

Power also may come from the *price*. The American Academy of Ophthalmology (AAO) charges domestic members $825 and international ones $485, both of which include registration at their annual conference. AAO is experimenting with an online-only membership of $100 for emerging economies. However, Jane Aguirre, CAE, vice president of global alliances at AAO, is concerned about losing some of the perceived value. "There is the perception when someone sees the electronic membership badge that this doctor is successful, at least in part, because he or she can afford our membership."

People will pay a premium for a strong brand. A Big Mac may cost half as much in Thailand as in the United States, but it is still more expensive than the analogous sandwich you'd get from a sidewalk vendor down the street. "When a level of perceived quality has been (or can be) created, raising the price not only provides margin dollars but also aids perceptions," according to *Brand Leadership* by David A. Aaker and Erich Joachimsthaler. "Strong brands command a premium price."

AT THE CENTER

A brand that functions as an association's central organizing principle is the strongest of all. Brand is the nucleus of the association.

"Your brand is the 'north star' for experience design," says Jeneanne Rae, president of Peer Insight, an Alexandria, Virginia-based consultancy. "If you don't understand what you stand for, it's very difficult to create a coherent member experience."

Brand generates increased awareness, loyalty, and revenues, but it must be managed strategically with full management and organizational buy-in. "There's no question that the board has to sign off on the organization's branding," Carolyn Patterson, president emeritus of Governance Matters told D.K. Holland, author of *Branding for Nonprofits*. But first, the board needs to be clear about the mission and vision of the organization in order to be able to give direction.

"Because the brand is an association or company's most important asset, the process of branding provides the direction, inspiration and energy for the brand itself," according to the style book of the National Association for College Admission Counseling.

Using the brand as a central organizing principle does several things:
- *Ensures a shared vision throughout the organization.* This is where brand brings the mission to life in ways that are both tangible and intangible. It encompasses all the various value propositions you take to market. What does your mission look like in practice? That's

your value proposition. What does your mission *feel* like? That's your brand. Scientific and academic associations issue calls for papers and hold conclaves and symposia. High-tech user groups hold workshops with technical specifications. Other B2B associations run PowerPoint presentations at conferences preceding golf outings. Every one of those is a brand decision that communicates who you are.

- *Provides a critical "litmus test" to decision-making.* Low-hanging fruit is a strong temptation. Money that walks in the door in the form of easy assignments with quick payoffs is hard to turn down. If the brand is your central organizing principle, however, and everyone thoroughly understands it, it's easy to turn down the wrong assignments, the ones that are inconsistent with the brand. For example, an association known for its work with very senior executives took on a large research project about AIDS. But the project was so inconsistent with the organization's brand that it went nowhere—did nothing to fulfill the association's mission or to raise the profile of the sponsoring company. "Michael Porter [author of *Competitive Strategy*] wrote everything that needs to be written about strategy," says Mark Langley, executive vice president and chief operating officer of the Project Management Institute. "He said it's everything you choose to do and everything you choose not to do."

- *Guides tactical and long-term strategy.* All brands evolve, of course. But it is difficult for any organization to maintain both day-to-day focus and the long-range view simultaneously. "The nonprofit world is chock-full of fuzzy brands," Holland says, "mostly because nonprofit organizations are too busy focusing on service delivery or fundraising to consider the core work of branding. Ironically, solid branding could help tremendously in these areas." A clear vision of a strong brand lets you see both what is right in front of you and where you are going.

- *Demands proactive rather than reactive thinking.* This is one of the biggest payoffs for associations. Notoriously risk-averse, slow-moving entities, associations too often lag behind market realities. Adhering to a brand strategy forces the board to be more proactive, to anticipate challenges and opportunities. It removes a lot of the confusion in the landscape and provides a clear view of what needs to be done.

TOUCH ME

Every interaction, every communication, every printed piece, every transaction is a touchpoint with your members and every one is your brand. The waiter at your annual dinner is as much a part of building your brand as your president. Each customer touchpoint is an opportunity to strengthen the brand and communicate its essence. "Within every brand touchpoint, there is a moment of truth," Peer Insight's Rae says. "The most powerful engagement happens when you can catch your member at that moment."

Your Web site and your publications, in many cases, constitute the brand all on their own. For a member who never attends a meeting, never joins a committee, never calls, the things you push at them comprise everything they know and feel about you. Those "mailbox members" renew for some reason. You can't find it in the value proposition. You might find it in the mission. Most likely you'll find it in the brand. They like you, as simple as that. You give them an experience—even at arm's length with a monthly magazine— that they enjoy.

"More than any other application, a Web site simulates the brand personality of a company," Wheeler writes. "Its palette of engaging content, sound, movement and color creates a walking, talking, interactive company experience. It's the next best thing to reality, and in some cases, it's more efficient, more user-friendly and faster. The customer is in charge."

Your Web site is the single most important branding tool you have today. It is where people will come first to learn about you. Both the tangible and the intangible must be apparent on your site. Are you a dynamic, progressive, innovative association? Do you understand your industry and your members? Can you be part of their daily lives in ways that will make them more productive and successful? "Your Web site should be as helpful, insightful and appealing to someone in Asia as it is to someone in Arizona," wrote Marilynn Mobley, senior vice president of Edelman, the world's largest independent public relations firm.

Rae cites an example of branding at a moment of truth while visiting Bank of America's Web site. She was trying to set up a savings account for her sons when up popped an automated wizard that said, "It looks like you're trying to open an account. Would you like some help?" The wizard walked her through a process that is repeated thousands of times a week and so can be automated with little staff involvement. "They got me at exactly the moment I was deciding to 'join,'" she says. Even though automated, the process felt more personal than drop-down menus and was completed in minutes. All her questions were answered, and she felt sure she had opened the right sort of account. The functionality of the Web site itself gave her a window into Bank of America.

Timeliness, interactivity, strong calls to action, and community work well on the Web. Print serves a different purpose, one that must be redefined in the Web 2.0 world. Magazines are tangible, portable, tactile. Articles are longer, more involved and in-depth. Design is lush, more visually inviting, memorable. Magazines have a longer shelf life than the ninety-second benchmark for Web site visits.

Using these two main touchpoints together, but in different ways, builds a solid brand foundation:

- The Web is timely, instant, always on, actionable, and interactive. With increased use of social media, it is used for community building.

- Print connotes consistency, depth, recall, image, and emotion.

Some associations, particularly those related to high-tech industries, can do away with their print publication because their audience prefers the online medium. IPC discontinued its quarterly print magazine, *Review*, in favor of an all-Web strategy that fits its international goals. But they are considering an annual publication in order to have something tangible, a leave-behind for conference attendees and a mailing to current and potential members. Others are using digital magazines to replicate the print experience for global audiences without the printing and postage costs. But for most, print remains a pillar of brand building and brand maintenance, especially in the absence of other advertising. It is the central brand experience for many, many members.

MULTIMEDIA

For years, probably since the concept of branding was invented, the way to communicate brand was through advertising. This is most likely where the confusion of the brand and the logo came into being. Something snappy and memorable, with a logo, a color palette, a tagline, maybe a jingle, and mountains of metrics on recall proved that advertising worked as a brand builder.

This worked against associations, which never were enthusiastic advertisers. But technology that allows consumers to opt out of seeing advertisements and current trends in brand communication play directly into the hands of associations that historically have been too busy living the brand to realize they had one. Associations are not wedded to media that fewer and fewer people pay attention to. And they already have an arsenal of touchpoints that allows for building a robust brand in today's multimedia world.

According to *BusinessWeek*'s annual ranking of the world's strongest brands, the best ones "focus ruthlessly on every detail of their brands, honing simple, cohesive identities that are consistent in every product, in every market around the world, and in every contact with consumers." And they do that "in a host of new venues: the Web, live events, cell phones, and handheld computers."

Such a multipronged approach is perfect for associations. They already have the touchpoints of live events, active personal networks, magazines and newsletters, and ongoing research projects that tap members for information.

The conventional wisdom on global branding was that it should be different country to country, even region to region. The idea was that social and cultural relevance, not to mention language, needed to be so matched to the audience that one size could not fit all. As companies have gained experience with globalization, however, that turns out not to be the case. The leaders use single brands everywhere in the world, according to *BusinessWeek*. "The goal today is to create consistency and impact, both of which are a lot easier to manage with a single worldwide identity. It's also a more efficient approach, since the same strategy can be used everywhere." Translation and localization may still be necessary, but as long as the experience is large enough for a global audience to embrace, the same Web page can work around the world. The home page of the Americas Association of Cooperative/Mutual Insurance Societies is split in half, English and Spanish. When you click on either English or Español, you go to one of two separate but identical home pages.

The trend that is altering brand campaigns most profoundly is the shift from reach (how many consumers see my ad) and frequency (how often they see it) to personalization. The strongest brands are those that get customers to invite them into their lives. Enthusiastic Listserv participants or members who use your online inventory tracking tool have invited your brand into their professional lives. Losing members after they attain certification, an all-too-common occurrence, is the exact point at which you cease to be invited into their lives. If you have nothing that matches their specific professional needs, you are expendable.

Databases and the reams of metrics gleaned from Web traffic can fuel a personalization campaign that makes your brand essential to members. You know what meetings they attend, what publications they buy, and what committees they belong to, not to mention where they work, what job they hold, what gender they are, and probably where they went to school. Take all of that and create a unique, personal experience for each member—each member, not large groups of members—that cuts through the clutter.

With 140,000 members, the American Society of Civil Engineers must guard against providing one-size-fits-all products and services. "No one wants to be treated like a number," says ASCE Executive Director Pat Natale. "We're totally reinventing our Web site. Our belief is that it should be like Amazon.com based on everything we know about them. They expect us to have the best."

Associations always will provide products and services that appeal to a broad cross section of the membership—the annual meeting, the monthly magazine, awards. "There's value in that," says Jeff De Cagna, founder of Principled Innovation, "everyone benefits from those." But there are also specialized areas—sometimes extremely specialized—that need to be explored more deeply. "As knowledge becomes more specialized, people are going to need to be able to find things," De Cagna says. "If we can aggregate those people into a marketplace, that's an opportunity." And it can be part of the brand experience because it will have the unique personal touch that only your association could add.

Social media's reliance on user-generated content allows members to go as deeply as they want. An extremely vertical, entirely personal experience for a self-selected group—"that's a viable alternative to membership," De Cagna says, "by growing the surface area of our associations, by making it easier for people to connect with one another and with the marketplace."

That increased surface area with many very deep, vertical niches constitutes a new brand for associations whose brand essence has always been tightly tied to membership. "We will never go away from the membership model," PMI's Langley says. "It's almost a core value." Separating the experience from an identity as a membership organization will be a real wrench, but it may be the only way forward. In many cases, associations need to switch from recruiting members to courting customers. Without the affiliation of membership, they must build brands that can be communicated clearly and quickly to anyone.

If the Society for Human Resource Management, for instance, exists to serve HR professionals, do those professionals have to be members? If SHRM can provide them with "the most current and comprehensive resources," do they have to join to get those? Or is it completely consistent with SHRM's brand to provide those in other ways to other constituencies?

Being a membership organization certainly is part of an association's brand. But as the membership model is deconstructed in the face of new market realities, what does that do to the brand? The value proposition must remain sustainable and repeatable even as it becomes more episodic. The onus moves to innovation, to proving your worth every day, to being responsive to the rapid changes members/customers face. The Corporate Executive Board, with a retention rate of 90 percent, develops four or five new programs, publishes twenty-five thousand "fast cycle" research requests, and has expanded individual participation to more than three programs annually. That is the sort of relentless innovation that adds power and sustainability to the brand.

KNOW THYSELF

"One of the biggest errors in judgment nonprofits make is thinking they *are* the audience—that they have an *innate* understanding of their audience," writes D.K. Holland in *Branding for Nonprofits*. For the International Interior Design Association, for example, "Our international development starts with being an outpost for American designers working internationally," says Cheryl Durst, IIDA's executive director. "There are so many of them working in places like Dubai. It trickles out from there."

But as soon as the trickling out begins, the audience has changed, and its perception of the brand has as well. "Extensive and ongoing surveying is the only way to understand profoundly whom the organization is serving," Holland writes, "and to understand how the organization is perceived."

Association members and staff alike say they have survey fatigue. Member satisfaction surveys, reader surveys, research surveys, trend surveys, not to mention polls on Web sites and in e-newsletters, ballots for leadership, grassroots attitudinal surveys during political campaigns—the whole process, once aimed at engaging members, now only turns them off. Part of the problem is that those asked don't feel as though they get much in return for their answers. Most of the problem comes from sheer volume.

The solution is two-fold.

- First, use online community and user-generated content to turn your Web site into a giant data feed. Then do something substantive with the data to constantly improve your offering and the value you provide.

- Second, use field research to discover latent needs while using surveys to address the explicit top-of-mind needs. By riding along with a member for a day, observing them in their zone as market researchers do, associations can learn what members might not even know they need—the wants they can't articulate because no one's thought of them yet.

An association is not a product, a use-it-and-forget-it intangible object. Association staff often complains about the passion of volunteer leaders, a passion that colors decision making and demands attention. That very passion is, however, what fuels associations. Members and other stakeholders are viscerally involved in the association's mission; they are part and parcel of the brand. Associations have some of the potentially strongest brands around because members pay to be part of them. "All members vote," ASCE's Natale says. "They vote when they pay their dues."

In most ways, associations should feel flattered by the intense competition they now confront. What they have—passionate members, myriad virtual and personal touchpoints, powerful missions—the competition must replicate before it can even start. Much of brand stewardship comes from acting on the power brand creates. Once a brand is clear, all it really needs is leadership.

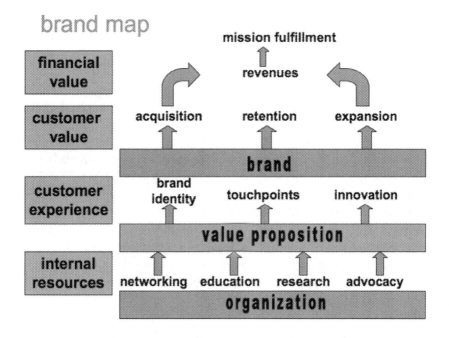

The association's internal resources are the foundation on which everything rests. If the infrastructure, business processes, and systems are not sound, there is little you'll be able to do in any case. The entire organization supports your value proposition, what you take to market, and all your product and service offerings. Those become the experiences that create your brand.

Customer experience includes your identity, logo, color palette, design, and so on—the "entry point" into your brand. This tends to come out of marketing and be the way potential members first notice you. They become aware of you through your brand identity, promotional materials, your Web site, etc., and that leads to acquisition.

Brand touchpoints are where you live the brand. These are the experiences that members have at meetings, within committees, or through your research and publications. The consistent, high-quality delivery of each touchpoint retains members. If members leave after they receive your credential, for instance, it is either because there are no new touchpoints for them, no other products and services, because the quality is lacking or, further down the map, because the value proposition offers them nothing beyond the credential itself. Innovation keeps the brand fresh and the value proposition compelling.

Brand expansion is the final area within brand. Up-sell, cross-sell, ancillary products, and new and different applications expand the member experience and expose members to new things and new thinking from the organization. "We are constantly on alert to the fact that a brand has a certain amount of elasticity," says ICF's Boyler.

All of that rolls up into revenues, to the financial stability that enables mission fulfillment.

Everything That Rises Must Converge

Each step toward creating a global brand builds on the last. Everything you do must roll up into fulfilling the mission. One thing changes, all things change. Tinkering with the organization, investing in brand identity, launching a global outreach effort to search for new revenues—none of these can happen in isolation. Any change that is small enough to leave the others unaffected is too timid in the current environment.

The Sincerest Form of Flattery

Successful brands are worth imitating because they are successful. McDonald's would not chase all of the quick-serve restaurants around the world that try to put a "Mc" in front of their menu if that perception of difference—of quality—were not there.

"The illegal spread of content usually means the legal spread of it is also going well," says Rohit Talwar, a futurist and CEO of Fast Future Ventures. "Thomas Friedman said he knew that *The World Is Flat* was popular when every third world taxi driver he rode with offered to sell him a knock-off copy."

If you ask an association executive about branding in global markets, they will talk about counterfeiting and intellectual property theft. "We have been selective in who we work with," says Kim Sterling, CAE, vice president of marketing at IPC, "and have used our attorneys where we find violations of our copyrights worldwide."

Associations must, of course, ensure that their brands, marks, and logos are legally protected in any new market.

"Where associations make a huge mistake is to think that the recourse and protections they have in the States exist overseas," says Terrance Barkan, founder of Association Management Services. "They underestimate the need for enforcement. Starbucks would never sign a deal with someone and then never go and check. Trust is good, control is better. Associations try to do globalization by signing deals with people without signing control mechanisms to make sure that things go as they should."

Protecting a brand globally goes far beyond making sure that a semblance of the association logo does not end up on someone else's certification. "Intellectual property protection: forget it," Talwar says. "In a global world, it's almost impossible to protect and you couldn't afford it if you wanted to try."

Questions from Bernd Schmitt, executive director of the Columbia Business School Center on Global Brand Leadership

- Is it really necessary to standardize brand icons and positioning?
- Do you necessarily need one public face—one spokesperson—for your brand?
- Is it essential to centralize organizational structures?

Myth versus Reality

Myth	Reality
Brand is something you own.	Members' views define brand reality.
Brands take care of themselves.	Branding is an ongoing, proactive pursuit.
Brand awareness equals relevance.	Awareness is only recall. Relevance comes from delivery on brand promise.
Our brand is fine and doesn't need any changes.	Internal arrogance, wishful thinking, and politics nullify the clarity that a strong brand strategy creates.
Branding is the marketing department's job.	Branding is everyone's job.

Chapter 6

Leadership

Le futur n'est plus ce qu'il était.

—Isaac Asimov

"The good news is there's a new president," says Gary Boyler, executive director of the International Coach Federation. "The bad news is there's a new president." The revolving door of association leadership may be the biggest single problem associations have to solve. The tension between staff and board consumes so much energy, produces so much useless paper, and entails so many endless meetings that it takes everyone's eye off the ball. When associations are accused of being slow-moving, unable to anticipate competitive challenges, and chronically risk-averse, the blame lies with how they are led.

The staff of an association, who are the people paid to run the place, sign up members, create programs, organize meetings, do research, lobby lawmakers, manage the Web site, and publish the magazine, are a dedicated group to be sure. Many have never worked in a for-profit, and far too many are used to a slow pace and an environment where no one sticks his neck out.

"Are we going to believe that incrementalism and optimizing the status quo are going to get the job done?" asks Jeff De Cagna, founder of Principled Innovation. "Or are we prepared to launch onto a trajectory that's fundamentally different? I believe it's got to be the latter."

Executive management is equally committed to the association sector. The Certified Association Executive (CAE) credential conferred by the American Society of Association Executives (ASAE) recognizes people who never intended to do anything but be the best at an association career. Their political skills often get in the way of their leadership skills, however, or even substitute for them.

Some executives may come from the membership. The executive director of the American Medical Association is himself a doctor, for instance. The executive director of American Society of Civil Engineers is an engineer. But they are not the association.

An association board should be a representative body, constituted in a way that represents either each stakeholder contingent, or each region, or another egalitarian mix. The fact is that boards often are made up of members who were persuaded to volunteer and, following the universal axiom about productivity, a third will do the work, a third will watch, and a third won't even show up.

"Back in the old days, 20 or 30 years ago, you had the leaders of industry on the board of associations, at the table at board meetings," says Pat Natale, CAE, executive director of the American Society of Civil Engineers (ASCE), and incoming president of the Council of Engineering and Scientific Society Executives. "You don't get that anymore. The skill sets of boards are more those of junior managers."

There are exceptions—plenty of them—but the buck still stops on the leadership's desk. Decisions not made, hard choices not taken, and bold directions not pursued all point to a lack of leadership. "Many an executive has felt about a board the way the Quaker spinster did about a husband," writes Cyril O. Houle in *Governing Boards*. "It takes a very good one to be better than none."

The governance structure in some associations is so bad that the leadership itself realizes the problem. "I can't tell you the name of the association," says Andy Steggles, chief information officer of the Risk and Insurance Management Society, "but it actually has formed a competing association based on a subset of member interests. The board is going to let them go head-to-head to see whether the new one, which has all power residing with the executive director, can beat the old one, which has the traditional structure."

WHOSE FAULT IS THIS?

The fault lies not with individuals—many of whom are full of energy and ideas and completely aware of how to combat competition—but with the governance process itself. Mark Langley, executive vice president and chief operating officer of the Project Management Institute (PMI), says that the relentless pace necessary to run a global association "is easier when you look at the volunteer passion. Some of them are devoting 20 hours a week of their own time."

Ideally, the staff is operational and the board is strategic: board-led, staff-managed. The board sets the direction and the staff implements. "This is just not so," says Brian O'Connell, former professor of citizenship and public service at Tufts University. It is, in fact, "the worst illusion ever perpetrated in the nonprofit field." It is too simplistic and does not even approach the political and human dynamics of the situation or the revolving door of volunteer leadership.

"We're in an intellectual property business," says Peter J. O'Neil, co-executive director of the American Industrial Hygiene Association (AIHA). "Intellectual property is not a commodity. You have to grow it, stroke it, pet it. If you lose it, you can't buy it back. It's about heart, not head. It takes a long, long time to win. We run ourselves like a business. It's my job to tell the board what I know, what I've learned about a given situation, to be straight with them. I have to let them decide and abide by what that decision is even if I disagree with it. But helping them reach the right decision, that's the leadership part of my job."

In some very large associations, managing the board is a full-time job. The board of IEEE numbers three hundred. Meetings are three times a year and last for seven days. For a federated association with 375,000 members in one hundred fifty countries participating in thirty-nine tactical societies and five technical councils, perhaps the board needs to be that big. The body is split into separate boards that report up to a twelve-member executive committee. But meeting preparation and post-meeting communications consume a lot of resources. In many associations, there is almost no discussion of the high cost of governance. That alone should get someone's attention.

The existing structure with its strategic-tactical split also produces an enormous amount of tension. There is no discussion longer among association professionals than the one about governance—although there seldom is much discussion of what governance actually does in a post–Sarbanes-Oxley world. Rather, the talk is a combination of complaining, grousing, shrugging, and eye-rolling about the board. The implication is: if the board would only behave as the staff wishes it to behave and make the decisions the staff wants it to make, everything would be fine. While it is true that some sand in the oyster is necessary to produce a pearl, this amount of complaint and finger pointing implies a situation that is highly counterproductive. Much staff time is actually expended in outmaneuvering the board. "The Machiavellian part of association management," O'Neil says, "is that the staff needs to be two steps ahead of the board. You need to anticipate where they're going."

Many staffers are smart people, strategic thinkers in their own right. Being relegated to an operational, implementation role galls many of them. To add insult to injury, board members rarely have any experience in running an association. They may be fantastic at managing a project or running a textile mill, retailing or practicing medicine, but how to make an association more competitive is not something they know.

"For the board member, it's part-time and there's no risk, no skin in the game," Terrance Barkan of Association Management Services (AMS) says. "The staff knows more than the board about the real issues."

The situation only gets worse from there. If the board is less than committed, less than the best, if the staff is more interested in holding onto their jobs than doing battle with the competition, if the executives are walking a political tightrope between stakeholders, lowest-common-denominator decisions are what you'll get. Reaching a consensus in that environment is actually pretty astonishing. Agreeing on a bold direction forward is beyond imagination.

"Four years ago, we realized that if we did not change, we would die," says O'Neil of AIHA. "We were a dysfunctional organization." The lack of trust between staff and board, among staff members, and among board members was preventing AIHA from growing or functioning. "We managed 42 percent turnover for about 18 months, and I say managed because we knew it would happen. We planned for that. We hired differently. The staff side changed significantly. The board side changed significantly. Since then, we have launched major databases and online libraries. We developed a student professionals track. We agreed that, from an international standpoint, we would concentrate on three countries: India, China and Mexico. We've accomplished so much since the reorganization."

LEADERSHIP CHOICES

In ASAE's Center for Association Leadership research study, *7 Measures of Success: What Remarkable Associations Do that Others Don't*, one of the key differentiators between a good association and a great one is the CEO as a broker of ideas. "The CEO's vision for the members and his or her ability to foster effective communications, shared vision and collaborative action across volunteer and staff structures is what is important," says the study, "not the CEO's vision for the association." The CEO should be "able to inspire and facilitate visionary thinking throughout the organization."

The worm in the apple is that one of the board's principal jobs is hiring the CEO and holding him or her to agreed benchmarks. A dysfunctional board is more likely to hire a toothless CEO or to manage him or her in a mercurial fashion that keeps him off balance and incapable of action.

Great leaders don't last long in that environment, and even the ones blessed with good boards face a constant burden of proof each time the board changes. "It takes guts, money and vision," Gary Rubin of the Society for Human Resource Management (SHRM) says. "I wouldn't be here still if the leadership wasn't as good as it is. Our board, our CEO, our executive team, that's really important to me. SHRM's success is not an accident."

Sustaining a strategic direction in a dysfunctional environment can be all but impossible.

When the Institute of Food Technologists began its initiative in China, for instance, Executive Vice President Barbara Byrd Keenan spent eighteen months engaging the board in a series of conversations in order to get them on board. "Why China? Why food technology? Why now," she says. "You need to manage your board's expectations. Make it clear that you're in it for the long haul."

"For an international strategy," AIHA's O'Neil says, "a three-year plan is a minimum commitment." It took four attempts before the AIHA board approved an international affiliate membership (one-fourth of domestic membership and electronic only).

That's eighteen months to two years to get to a decision that will carry through for a minimum of three years and may see very low returns for quite a while. AIHA is on its third international taskforce, still searching for the ROI on global efforts. Selling it, reselling it, justifying it, proving it will work, and arguing that corner is an exhausting, seemingly endless process, the energy for which could be better used in making it happen. In the meantime, the window of opportunity may have closed with someone else having stepped into the void.

"We changed our governance in 1999," PMI's Langley says. "After that, the cyclicality ended." PMI board meetings, once characterized by chair throwing, settled down to make sure that the organization was positioned for the future. "My take on how the board works is: discussion, deliberation, decision. The staff is involved with the board in the first two and then the board decides."

Coincidentally, when PMI changed its governance and stopped the cyclicality, its growth spurt started. Since 1999, PMI has experienced 145 percent growth, mostly driven by globalization. Sustaining that growth is something of which Langley is confident. There are ten million people in the world who work in project management; only a quarter of a million are members of PMI. "Project management is about change," Langley says, "about getting things done. That's growth." One of the things that PMI has realized is that in the unbundled world of selling products rather than memberships, "associations may need a different funding model going forward. But that might be all you need to change."

This is not to say that boards should give the CEO a blank slate. There have been as many high-profile examples of lax oversight in the nonprofit world as in the for-profit. But it is to argue that selecting that CEO—one the board can trust—and then getting out of his or her way is the single most important thing an association board can do.

COMPETENCE

Association boards are not going away. The tripartite structure of board, staff, and members is not going away. Two things that *are* going away are parliamentary procedures and constituent-based boards, according to *The Will to Govern Well*.

The parliamentary process and consensus decision making can render association boards very slow moving and reinforce or even disguise the excess of caution that hampers decision making. In other words, parliamentary process adds no value and eats up time, according to the book. The highly structured process dictated by Robert's Rules of Order stifles productive brainstorming and reduces complex issues to motions with simple aye or nay answers.

Decisions no longer are based on simple consensus. "Base decisions on principles rather than passions," AMS's Barkan says.

The consensus model favors the most persuasive—or possibly just the loudest—rather than the best informed. It is, according to *The Will to Govern Well*, "opinion rich and knowledge poor." As more and more boards realize that complex issues have many answers and unanimity is impossible, they must base their decisions on knowledge—knowledge of the issues, of the competitive landscape, of the threats, and of the opportunities.

IEEE has moved to a data-driven decision-making model, which has streamlined meetings and made them operate more efficiently, according to Jim Vick, publisher and editorial director of IEEE Media. The association's Envisioned Future Strategy Initiative began in late 2007. It already has altered board agendas and meeting processes with the goal of ensuring that the board is a strategic entity which engages in issues that affect IEEE and its members, focuses governance on outcomes rather than actions, and leverages the intellectual capital of IEEE's leadership.

Given the difficulties of attracting volunteer leaders, not to mention the best leaders, moving to knowledge-based decision making actually can improve the quality of decisions even in the face of less-than-stellar decision makers. The process itself creates continuity from board to board that is missing when decisions are based on passion rather than information.

Cheryl Durst, executive director of the International Interior Design Association, runs her monthly conference calls with the board using a consent agenda. Materials are sent to the board in advance so, rather than getting bogged down in a presentation of the findings and a debate about them, the board can simply vote its consent and move on to the next item.

"The beauty of it is that anything can be moved out of the consent agenda at any time," says Jocelyn Pysarchuk, former director of communications at IIDA. "But it enabled us to move through a lot of stuff in 90 minutes."

More and more boards are becoming competency-based, what Barkan calls "a very evolved model," rather than constituency-based. "It's more effective," he says. "It will usually give you more talent, more commitment."

A competency-based board recognizes talent wherever it resides within the membership. It is also more likely to attract people who know what they're talking about. They may not know how to run an association, but they will know a lot about standards or finance or information technology. There should be a shared base of knowledge with staff in charge of those areas, and so a shared base of respect. Once the competencies are defined, executives can look for subject matter experts and are not constrained by geography, industry vertical, or anything else. It should also improve the quality of meetings, make better use of volunteers' time, and thus, make members more likely to volunteer.

Constituency-based boards must take what they can get in order to maintain voices from every corner. "Objectivity, fairness, consistency, that's what you're after," PMI's Langley says, "and change is not greeted well."

Competency-based boards and knowledge-based decision making factor strongly into how an association grooms future board members. They attract more sophisticated members rather than creating an automatic ladder of advancement through committees and special interest groups.

There are many associations that have tried and failed to create this more productive board structure. In the same way that water seeks its own level, some associations do the study, decide how they should change, and then revert to the old, familiar formula. The dysfunction is not bad enough, apparently. "I have no idea why associations are so slow to change," says SHRM's Rubin.

"I suppose it's because moving forward is a lot harder than standing still. They sacrifice a vibrant tomorrow to have a comfortable today."

In the association world, *The Will to Govern Well* says, knowledge leads to trust, which leads to nimbleness. Few individual members seriously consider whether they can trust the association's leadership, staff, or volunteers. They only know when the association ceases to meet their needs, at which time they wander off in ones and twos or even hundreds to more responsive sources. Leadership was not nimble enough to anticipate their needs, did not have a clear understanding of the association's purpose, and spent more time fighting with each other than getting on with the central mission of the whole enterprise.

"Every organization should reinvent itself every year," Langley says. "Associations control a domain. They've never had to deal with competition. If you don't reinvent yourself, you end up tweaking the model you've already got rather than really changing to fit the market."

At AIHA, the issue has moved from growth to right-sizing. "This is not a growing profession," O'Neil says. "We're now talking about right-sizing the membership. What we've seen in our survey results is that we haven't been able to grow. We've grown in revenues, grown our reserves, but not in membership, not in publication sales. We're spending a lot of energy and passion around ancillary industrial hygiene things. So is bigger really better?"

This is the leadership challenge that associations face. It is reinvention, not incremental change. It is not for the faint of heart.

COMMON SENSE

At the end of 2007, Booz Allen Hamilton published a report as part of its Resilience series. Called *Exercising Common Sense*, the report lays out ten critical factors that leaders can use when dealing with major transformation. The study shows that even when the need for major transformation is clear, CEOs find it difficult to keep a sharp focus on what needs to be done. This is largely due to uncertainty and to the conflicting messages that will inevitably lead to. It should not lead to what Jeff De Cagna calls FUD—fear, uncertainty, and doubt. The major transformation necessary for associations is an opportunity to be embraced rather than feared, and the self-doubt it creates may be one way to separate those that are up to the task from those who are not.

The authors of *Exercising Common Sense* used that title because the ten factors are "as vital as common sense suggests they should be." Those ten factors are the following:

1. The CEO makes a strong case for change by clearly and persuasively articulating the factors that are driving it.

2. Senior leaders set an aggressive, enterprise-wide target. Big goals are the key to driving big actions.

3. Senior management is firmly aligned.

4. An integrated enterprise-wide program for change is put in place.

5. Senior leaders focus on augmenting capabilities along with cutting costs.

6. "Moments of truth" are recognized and shared in order to demonstrate commitment.

7. A detailed plan provides the blueprint.

8. Enabling triggers are built in from the start.

9. Communication is proactive and ongoing.

10. The results of change are sustained.

"Achieving long-term results requires a sustained and focused leadership that transcends management formulas. The leaders who realize success tend to be uncommonly disciplined," says the report, "not just in the way they lead others, but in the way they govern themselves."

Sounds simple. But in an age of increasing globalization, spectacular technological advances, and shifting demographics, associations must take heed or they will have nothing left to govern. Their constituencies are losing patience, and the competition is hungry. In many cases and in many ways, the constituents are the competition.

The Golden Mean

"The principle of the golden mean applies with striking relevance to the work of board members. It is essential that they do enough but not too much, that they deliberate at sufficient length but not too long, that they are forceful when necessary but quiet when they should be, that they hold fast to what they believe but are not obstinate, and that they share their knowledge but do not spout it forth at excessive length."

—Cyril O. Houle, *Governing Boards*

Chapter 7

Conclusion

The center can not hold.

—William Butler Yeats

"Information is the lifeblood of every association," writes Susan E. Fox, CAE, in the *Journal of Association Leadership.*

"Membership development is the lifeblood of associations," says Kellen Company, an association management firm, on its Web site.

Responsibility, trust, committees, grassroots leadership, members, volunteers, and meetings all are described as the lifeblood of associations.

It is always written that way: boldly, a simple, declarative sentence with so much confidence and, admittedly, more than a little truth, to seem inarguable. You say to yourself, "Ah, that's what makes them tick."

But why talk about lifeblood? People are searching for the *one thing* that will keep associations going. The field of associations is a multibillion-dollar field, so they're not going away tomorrow. But smart association leaders know that the competition is different today—there's more of it, from many more sources and in many more forms. The twin forces of globalization and technology that revolutionized how successful companies compete represent a threat, but also an opportunity that associations must embrace.

AND NOW WHAT?

While this book has dealt primarily with the past and present states of associations in the world, it carries at its heart a warning that the future will be different. But how different, and in what ways? While the future never is easy to predict, I will speculate—make a better-than-average guess—based on all that I've learned from years of working with associations and months spent writing this book.

Association consolidation will continue and may accelerate. There are too many small associations that are simply unsustainable given the pressures on their business model and the shift of economic growth to new countries.

New associations will form. It will be much easier to start from scratch than to retrofit dysfunctional associations. Those that are determined to stick to the old ways of working—those with boards who can't or won't lead, those that can't muster strong enough consensus to plot a way forward—will simply wind down. It won't be pretty and it won't be quick, but it will happen. The new associations will be organized to fit the economic and membership realities of a new world order. Not married to the past, they'll be nimble and responsive. And most importantly, they'll do everything possible to ensure that members themselves are part of every conversation and every decision at every available opportunity.

Domestic associations won't go away but will form chains of federation that, in the largest sense, will make them global. Unless an association's brief is local or regional, all B2B associations will be global. There is an enormous talent gap, especially in the fast-growing BRIC (Brazil, Russia, India, China) countries, that associations can be a big part of filling. That's an opportunity not to be missed.

As the current generation retires, associations will be staffed by younger, technology-agnostic people. One of the wonderful things about technology is the law of unintended consequences—the cell phone was invented to make telecommunications portable, not to take pictures or help organize political rallies. Those young, savvy staff members who embrace technology rather than fear it will transform associations in ways that no one can predict. They may, in fact, be associations' salvation vis-à-vis the competition within.

Successful associations will rediscover their true competitive edge, the value proposition that cannot be replicated: they will stand for something. Most members desperately want to make a difference. (Corporate social responsibility is the number-one topic college students ask recruiters about potential employers.) Bringing together large numbers of people around a single, worthwhile purpose that has nothing to do with personal gain or profit is what makes associations special.

That's it—my best predictions. I've been to New York, Philadelphia, Madrid, Brussels, Warsaw, Stockholm, Washington DC, and Minneapolis, all in the last six months. I've met wildly committed people who see the future very clearly and ones that seem to look only through rear-view mirrors. I feel certain that the assumptions I've made and the conclusions I've reached in this book are correct even though they were, for me, entirely unexpected when I started to write.

Forget coziness and insularity. Talk to a lot of people—people outside your comfort zone—and listen. Associations are institutionalized networking. Use that skill to figure out where you're headed.

IN SUMMARY

Obstacles that make it difficult for associations to compete:

- The "we've always done it that way" mindset.

- Risk aversion.

- Painfully slow decision making.

- Bloated bureaucracies—staff, and boards, in some cases.

- Chauvinism—of nations, of industries, of professions—verging on hubris.

- Lack of resources or the misallocation of resources to outmoded, underperforming assets.

- The need to control the agenda.

- The tendency toward an inward focus and a resulting lack of openness.

- Lack of responsiveness and flexibility.

The built-in advantages of associations that will put them ahead of competitive forces:

- The ability to make the world a better, safer place for all mankind.

- The wisdom of crowds. Associations had it before everyone else started talking about it.

- User-generated content (same as above) in the form of volunteer contributions to research, education, communications, event planning, standards development, and professionalism. And today, also contributions to wikis, Listservs, social communities.

- Passion—an intense commitment to the group's value proposition.

- Camaraderie—not to be dismissed in a *Bowling Alone* world.

- The cross-pollination of ideas in an open, trusted forum.

- The invaluable network of peers.

  The business models of most associations must be reinvented:

- The dues-based membership model is unsustainable in the face of the unbundling necessary to globalization, demographic changes, and competition from no-dues options online.

- The pay-for-access model is unsustainable in an increasingly open-access world.

- The advertising model is unsustainable in an era of dying print products and the smaller amounts that digital is currently returning, plus the difficulty of monetizing rich media opportunities.

- The meeting attendance model may be sustainable but will come under increasing threat from virtual events and the lower amounts that smaller, more local and regional meetings can command.

- The research model is sustainable but will be undermined by open access.

  Associations can meet the new competitive pressures, but they must figure out new ways to get paid. What will people pay for, and how much? People will pay for:

- Strategic thinking. Associations can become more consultative and less programmatic.

- Inside information. Associations always have excelled at research and can compete for contract-research projects that entail deep involvement with constituents.

- Access. Associations must figure out what to keep proprietary and what to open up.

- Exclusivity. Associations can convene tightly focused groups in off-the-record settings that will result in both inside information and a sense of exclusivity.

- A role in making the world a better place. Standards-setting, credentialing, and advocacy can be the true competitive advantage of certain associations. There is, of course, a limit to this. The proliferation of professional letters parked behind a name must stand for something substantive or they'll become like college degrees you can buy online.

- Communications. Media that creates engagement that leads to action will always pay for itself. Creating engagement is more difficult than creating information overload. This no longer is a one-way communication that associations control. They can not simply push information at recipients and call it communications.

- The opportunity to come together—preferably someplace wonderful. Associations increasingly will capitalize on one of the main reasons that people come to events and the only one that cannot be replicated online: fabulous locations. The quality of the content must remain the primary pull, but that will be coupled with well-managed entertainment specific to the audience.

- Career advancement. Research proves that successful people join associations in order to become more successful. Being the place where those people meet, network, find new jobs, and close deals is another huge competitive advantage of associations.

- Help in managing complexity. The future will bring increasingly blurred lines between the personal and the professional sides of life. Helping members manage their lives in a holistic sense is an opportunity few associations have yet exploited.

Reinvention is more than using new technology to produce more of the same. Associations must consider a major, top-to-bottom transformation that will catapult them into new, unchartered competitive space. In a borderless world, *the ability to reinvent themselves* will be the lifeblood of associations.

Associations

Associations included in research for this book and/or contacted for data, information and interviews:

Academy of Certified Hazardous Materials Managers (ACHMM), www.achmm.org

American Academy of Ophthalmology (AAO), www.aao.org

American Anthropological Association (AAA), www.aaanet.org

Americas Association of Cooperative/Mutual Insurance Societies (AACMIS) www.aacmis.org

American Bankers Association (ABA), www.aba.com

American Business Media (ABM), www.americanbusinessmedia.com

American Chemical Society (ACS), www.acs.org

American Chemistry Council (ACC), www.americanchemistry.com

American Composites Manufacturers Association (ACMA), www.acmanet.org

American Health Information Management Association (AHIMA), www.ahima.org

American Heart Association (AHA), www.americanheart.org

American Industrial Hygiene Association (AIHA), www.aiha.org

American Medical Association (AMA), www.ama-assn.org

American Planning Association (APA), www.planning.org

American Plastics Council (APC), www.americanchemistry.com/plastics

American Society of Association Executives (ASAE), www.asaecenter.org

American Society for Cell Biology (ASCB), www.ascb.org

American Society of Clinical Oncology (ASCO), www.asco.org

American Society of Civil Engineers (ASCE), www.asce.org

American Society of Interior Designers (ASID), www.asid.org

American Society of Mechanical Engineers (ASME), www.asme.org

American Society for Quality (ASQ), www.asq.org

American Society for Therapeutic Radiology and Oncology (ASTRO), www.astro.org

American Society of Training and Development (ASTD), www.astd.org

Association of American Publishers (AAP/PSP), www.publishers.org

Association of Collegiate Business Schools and Programs (ABCSP), www.acbsp.org

Boy Scouts of America (BSA), www.scouting.org

Chemical Industrial Sector Advisory Committee

China Association for Quality, www.caq.org.cn

Chinese Institute of Food Science and Technology (CIFST), www.cifst.org.cn/en

The Conference Board, www.conference-board.org

Corporate Executive Board, www.executiveboard.com

Council of Engineering and Scientific Society Executives (CESSE), www.cesse.org

EduCAUSE, www.educause.edu

Emergency Nurses Association (ENA), www.ena.org

Girl Scouts of America (GSA), www.girlscouts.org

Healthcare Financial Management Association (HFMA), www.hfma.org

IEEE, www.ieee.org

Institute of Food Technologists (IFT), www.ift.org

Institute of Internal Auditors (IIA), www.theiia.org

International Association of Scientific, Technical & Medical Publishers (STM), www.stm-assoc.org

International Coach Federation (ICF), www.coachfederation.org

International Interior Design Association (IIDA), www.iida.org

International Society of Nephrology (ISN), www.nature.com/isn

IPC (Association Connecting Electronics Industries), www.ipc.org

Metals Service Center Institute (MSCI), www.msci.org

Million Dollar Round Table (MDRT), www.mdrt.org

National Association for College Admission Counseling (NACAC), www.nacacnet.org

National Association of Corporate Directors (NACD), www.nacdonline.org

National Association of Wholesaler-Distributors (NAW), www.naw.org

Professional Photographers of America (PPA), www.ppa.com

Project Management Institute (PMI), www.pmi.org

Public Affairs Council (PAC), www.pac.org

Regulatory Affairs Professionals Society (RAPS), www.raps.org

Risk and Insurance Management Society Inc. (RIMS), www.rims.org

Rotary International, www.rotary.org

Security Industry Association (SIA), www.siaonline.org

Society for Human Resource Management (SHRM), www.shrm.org

Synthetic Organic Chemical Manufacturers Association (SOCMA), www.socma.com

U.S. Chamber of Commerce, www.uschamber.com

Virginia Association of REALTORS, www.varealtor.com

Sources

Aaker, David A. and Joachimsthaler, Erich. *Brand Leadership*. Simon & Schuster, 2002

Anderson, Chris. *The Long Tail; Why the Future of Business is Selling More of Less*. Hyperion, 2006

Association Meeting Analysis 2007. IMEX Research.

Association Publishing Benchmarking Study. Angerosa Research Foundation. 2005

Association Publishing Survey. Folio and Readex Research, 2006 and 2007

Barabási, Albert-László. *Linked*. Plume, 2003

Best Practices in Virtual Events. FactPoint Group, 2007

Burt, Ronald S. *Structural Holes versus Network Closure as Social Capital*, 2000

Cross, Rob and Parker, Andrew. *The Hidden Power of Social Networks: Understanding How Work Really Gets Done in Organizations*. Harvard Business School Press, 2004

The Decision to Join. American Society of Association Executives & The Center, 2007

2008 Digital Future Project. USC Annenberg School Center for the Digital Future, 2008

Drucker, Peter. *Managing in the Next Society*. St Martin's Griffin, 2002

E-Publishing Trends & Metrics. Angerosa Research Foundation, 2007

2006 Executive Compensation & Benefits Study. American Society of Association Executives & The Center

Exercising Common Sense, Booz Allen Hamilton. 2007

Five Independent Thinkers (Jeff De Cagna, David Gammel, Jamie Notter, Mickie Rops, Amy Smith). *101 Things About Associations We Must Change.* Lulu Enterprises, Inc., 2006

The Future of the Competitive Association. U.S. Chamber of Commerce, 2005

Generations and the Future of Association Participation. William E. Smith Institute for Association Research, 2006

Holland, D.K, *Branding for Nonprofits.* Allworth Press, 2006

Houle, Cyril. *Governing Boards: Their Nature and Nurture.* Jossey-Bass, 1997

Kleinberg, Jon, et al. *Group Formation in Large Social Networks: Membership, Growth and Evolution,* 2006

Lenskold, James D. *Marketing ROI: The Path to Campaign, Customer, and Corporate Profitability.* McGraw-Hill, 2003

Li, Yuwen, editor. *Freedom of Association in China and Europe.* Martinus Nijhoff Publishers, 2005

Mapping the Future of Your Association. American Society of Association Executives & The Center, 2006

McConnell, Ben and Huba, Jackie. *Creating Customer Evangelists: How Loyal Customers Become a Volunteer Salesforce.* Kaplan Business, 2003

Membership Recruitment and Retention in Europe. The Association Gateway, 2006

Moore, Geoffrey. *Crossing the Chasm.* Collins Business, 2002

On the Web, Some Countries Matter More than Others. Common Sense Advisory, 2007

Operating Ratio Report, 13th edition. American Society of Association Executives & The Center

Policies and Procedures in Association Management, Volume 1. American Society of Association Executives & The Center, 2006

Porter, Michael E. *The Competitive Advantage of Nations.* Free Press, 1990

Promoting Your Credentials in Faraway Places. American Society of Association Executives & The Center, 2004

Rheingold, Howard. *The Virtual Community; Homesteading on the Electronic Frontier.* The MIT Press, first published in 1993, republished in 2000

Shirkey, Clay. *Here Comes Everybody; The Power of Organizing without Organizations.* Penguin Press HC, 2008

Smith, Marc A. and Kollock, Peter. *Communities in Cyberspace.* Routledge, 1999, republished 2004

Strategic Review on Association Development: International Trends, Issues and Options. Association Global Services, 2006

The State of the News Media 2008. Project for Excellence in Journalism.

Tecker, Glenn H., Frankel, Jean S., Meyers, Paul D. *The Will to Govern Well.* American Society of Association Executives, 2002

Teten, David and Allen, Scott. *The Virtual Handshake: Opening Doors and Closing Deals Online.* AMACOM, 2005

Wheeler, Alina. *Designing Brand Identity: A Complete Guide to Creating, Building, and Maintaining Strong Brands.* Wiley, 2003

Where the Winners Meet. William E. Smith Institute for Association Research, 2008

Index

American Plastics Council, 25

American Society of Association
    Executives (ASAE), 2, 3, 10,
    27, 90

American Society for Cell Biology,
    56

American Society of Civil
    Engineers (ASCE), 15, 71,
    90

American Society of Interior
    Designers (ASID), 7, 8

American Society of Mechanical
    Engineers (ASME), 29

American Society for Quality
    (ASQ), 6, 11, 21

Anderson, Chris, 4, 39, 60

ASAE, *see* American Society of
    Association Executives
    (ASAE)

ASQ, *see* American Society for
    Quality (ASQ)

Association of American
    Publishers, 56

Association Connecting Electronics
    Industries (IPC), 68

Association Growth Partners, 51,
    59, 76

Association of Collegiate Business
    Schools and Programs
    (ACBSP), 11

Associations
  consolidation, 100
  cultural relevance, 6
  dependability, 76
  future of, 100–101
  growth, 6, 10, 12, 21
  identity, 21
  international, 17, 22
  joining, 3, 5–7
  local, 2, 8, 9, 17, 81, 100
  loyalty to, 62, 66, 77
  mission, 2, 59, 76
  professional, 25, 66
  relevance, 8–10, 18, 20, 21
  scientific, 40
  small, 39
  social responsibility, 100
  trade, 7, 23, 25, 66, 68
  transformation, 96–97
  trust, 6, 7
  unbundling, 18, 20, 60

Associations Matter, 18

facilitators, 57

languages, 34

strong ties, 46

user-generated content, 50, 82

Operations, 19

costs of, 60

Rich media, *see* digital media

Risk and Insurance Management
Society (RIMS), 39, 53, 66,
90

Rotary International, 1, 2, 8–9

S

Security Industry Association (SII),
66

Services, 4, 15, 67, 68; *see also*
value propositions

Shirky, Clay, 2

Smith Institute, *see* William E.
Smith Institute

Social capital, 7, 46

Social media, *see* online
communities

Social networks, 2, 10, 38, 39; *see
also* online communities

research on, 5–6

sites, 10

Social responsibility, 25, 71, 100

Society for Human Resource
Management (SHRM), 21,
28, 44, 70

Special interest groups (SIGs), 2,
14, 64, 95

Staff, *see* governance

Standards, 4, 29–30, 49, 68

T

Technology, 10, 18; *see also* digital
media

keeping up with, 44–45

opportunities, 52

value, 45

Trade associations, 7, 23, 25, 66,
68

Training, 27, 54

TrendHunter, 67

Tucker, Glenn, 22

Twitter, 50

U

U.S. Chamber of Commerce, 4, 5

V

Value propositions, 2, 66–68

beyond individuals, 6

competition, 66

components of, 59–60

differentiation, 67

empowerment, 67

in Europe, 73